791.43652
A547m

AGF-5143
Ø2.95
m=26

D1030438

Mammies No More

Mammies No More

The Changing Image
of Black Women
on Stage and Screen

Lisa M. Anderson

ROWMAN & LITTLEFIELD PUBLISHERS, INC.
Lanham • Boulder • New York • Oxford

ROWMAN & LITTLEFIELD PUBLISHERS, INC.

Published in the United States of America
by Rowman & Littlefield Publishers, Inc.
4720 Boston Way, Lanham, Maryland 20706

12 Hid's Copse Road
Cummor Hill, Oxford OX2 9JJ, England

Copyright © 1997 by Rowman & Littlefield Publishers, Inc.

British Library Cataloguing in Publication Information Available

Library of Congress Cataloging-in-Publication Data

Anderson, Lisa M., 1966—
    Mammies no more : the changing image of Black women on stage and
screen / Lisa M. Anderson.
        p.   cm.
    Includes bibliographical references and index.
    ISBN 0-8476-8419-9 (alk. paper)
    1. American drama—20th century—History and criticism.   2. Women
and literature—United States—History—20th century.   3. Afro-
American women in motion pictures.   4. Afro-American women in
literature.   5. Afro-Americans in motion pictures.   6. Afro-
Americans in literature.   I. Title.
PS338.W6A53   1997
791.43′652042′08996073—dc21   97-9782
                                                                  CIP

ISBN 0-8476-8419-9 (cloth : alk. paper)

Printed in the United States of America

⊗ ™ The paper used in this publication meets the minimum requirements of
American National Standard for Information Sciences—Permanence of Paper for
Printed Library Materials, ANSI Z39.48-1984.

This work is dedicated to all of the black women
in my life, especially my Mom, my sisters Leah and Lori,
and my dear friends Tina and Valerie, who continually
remind me that we are more than the images they make of us.

Contents

Acknowledgments

A great many people have helped me in the development of this work. At the University of Washington, I was guided by the dedication and persistence of the School of Drama doctoral faculty, especially Sarah Bryant-Bertail and Barry Witham. Before his death in 1994, Michael Quinn provided me with the necessary theoretical basis and a belief in my abilities. Tina Redd and Valerie Curtis-Newton sustained me through the completion of the project. Jason Rubis encouraged, edited, and suffered through late-night theorizing of the first draft.

I am also grateful for the support of my colleagues at Purdue. Renee White, Carolyn Johnson, Floyd Hayes, James Bell, and Anthony Zamora listened to chapters in various stages of development. Lewis Gordon read a draft of the entire manuscript and gave me invaluable advice and encouragement. The Women's Studies Program provided me space to present some of my ideas, as did the African American Studies and Research Center. My colleagues in the Theatre Department have also strongly supported my efforts, and I thank them for their patience.

I am indebted to Liz Fugate, the University of Washington Libraries; the Performing Arts Library–Lincoln Center; the Schomberg Library; the Film Stills Archive at the Museum of Modern Art; and the Humanities, Social Science, and Education Library at Purdue for their assistance in gathering scripts, materials, and photographs. I am also grateful to Scarecrow Video for access to videotapes of the films, and to the Seattle Group Theatre for the use of production photographs. I would also like to thank the Dorothy Danforth Compton Graduate Fellows Program, which sponsored two years of my work. Finally, I appreciate the love and support of my family.

Introduction

Reflections of Our Lives

We need to see the reflections of our own personal lives to give them meaning, and to assuage our fears.

—Paula Giddings, *Where and When I Enter: The Impact of Black Women on Race and Sex in America*

This study explores some of the cultural representations of black women with the question, why is it that black women are perceived in certain, recurring ways, and are expected to have certain characteristics, ideologies, and behaviors? Because the cultural representations of black women are not abundant, none of them can be thought of as "just *a* black woman." The racial stratification of the United States ensures that there are many communities in this country whose only exposure to black people is through the media. Media representations, as the only ones, form these people's conceptions of blacks. If there are a few blacks within these communities, they are anomalies, defying expectations. They are "complimented" by their white neighbors with statements such as "I don't think of you as a black person." The stage or screen image stands for black women in a way the token blacks in the office, or down the street, cannot. Thus, the white American interpretation of the black woman, as she is projected onto stage and screen, becomes the so-called real black. Think, for example, of the liberal critique of *The Cosby Show* as an "unrealistic" depiction of a black family (see chapter 4).

This interpreted "black woman" becomes an icon, in the semiotic sense, as Jean Alter discusses in *A Sociosemiotic Theory of Theatre* (1990); "black woman," whether mammy, tragic mulatta, or jezebel, refers to her mirror image in the space off the stage or screen. The stage mirror is supposedly reflecting the image of a real black woman in the audience or somewhere in the real world but is in fact reflecting an imaginary woman—that fictional "black woman" who has been created. The icon "black woman" is both a primary and a cultural sign; the figure that appears on stage refers to a person, ostensibly in the audience but certainly somewhere in the world, who is being reflected on stage. Alter's metaphor clarifies the complex relationship between the represented and the repre- sentation: "Even the best mirrors distort a little, but even the worst mirrors retain exceptionally high iconicity" (1990: 98). This icon, "black woman," comes to stand for all black women; the image is fixed in such a way that it affects all other representations and real people.

To challenge a prevailing icon successfully, there must be a large number of contrasting images (or enough personal contact to deuniversalize the real human beings behind the icons) in conjunc- tion with other sociological, economic, and political changes. Since the nineteenth century, black artists, both male and female, have attempted to present contrasting and alternative images in order to change the sign (icon) of black women, which has been confined in representation to a few demeaning and largely unrealistic images. The mammy, the tragic mulatta, and the jezebel are three of the most pervasive and most popular images and the ones that will be explored in this book. The twentieth century has witnessed an increasingly dedicated effort to replace those images with more di- versified, realistic images.

In 1916, Angelina Weld Grimke submitted the manuscript of her play, *Rachel*, to the Committee on the Drama of the Washing- ton, D.C., branch of the NAACP. This committee, whose member- ship included Alain Locke, NAACP Vice President Archibald H. Grimke (Angelina's father), and Montgomery Gregory, was charged with selecting a play that would be the first written by an

2

African American to be produced as a protest. The play functioned as both Grimke's and the NAACP's response to the distribution of D. W. Griffith's 1915 film, *The Birth of a Nation*. Based on a novel about the origins of the Ku Klux Klan, the film's presentations of blacks were inaccurate and demeaning, and they served to spread the influence and strengthen the numbers of the Klan. Grimke's play showed the plight of African Americans, which involved being restricted to menial labor and little opportunity. *Rachel* followed in a tradition of blacks resisting and attempting to change white-produced images of themselves. During the nineteenth century, groups of black minstrels attempted to reclaim the minstrel form. They changed some of the characters and songs, moved the emphasis away from the happy slave to the freed man, and incorporated more of their own culture, such as Jubilee songs, into the act. Unfortunately, the icons of minstrelsy that had been formed by whites in blackface were too entrenched for such changes to affect those images (see Anderson 1996). In the continuing effort to affect and effect social and political change, African American artists and intellectuals sought the transformation of the representations of African Americans, including stage and screen images.

People of African descent had held a place in the theatrical imagination of white Westerners before Griffith's film, or even before white minstrel performer Thomas "Daddy" Rice created his minstrel character Jump Jim Crow. William Shakespeare's *Othello* dramatizes the primitive violence of those with dark skin; Caliban, of *The Tempest*, is the Other who rapaciously desires white women and attempts in vain to challenge the authority of white men. These images are not alone. The imagined lives of people of African descent continue to be dramatized in Western culture as fact. Seldom positive, they are usually inaccurate depictions of the lives of blacks.

By the nineteenth century in the United States, the Euro-Americans' images of blacks were influenced primarily by the institution of slavery. Whites expressed their impressions of blacks through the minstrel show, which showed blacks as happy slaves, amusing performers, and uneducated savages. For example, the African Grove Company, an early nineteenth-century group of black actors who staged Shakespearean as well as contemporary drama, was satirized by white theatre managers, as Samuel Hay chronicles in his *African American Theatre: An Historical and Critical Analysis* (1994). Even when American drama turned from the melodramatic and the minstrel traditions toward realism, the icons, codified by years of misrepresentation, did not change substantially.

The shift to realism in American drama might have facilitated a change in dramatic representations of blacks in mainstream theatre, but as we will see, little did change. Throughout the twentieth century, the images derived from minstrelsy and images of blacks as they were seen through the eyes of whites continued to create and reinforce stereotypes about African Americans. These portrayals weren't realistic but belonged in the realm of fiction and fantasy. We will explore some of the choices about representation, particularly self-representation, that have faced African American women playwrights as they have attempted to recreate and revise black representation.

Specifically, we will focus on three of the primary representations of African American women, as they appeared in dramas by both white and black playwrights. Both their positive and negative representations are examined, as well as the historical circumstances that created and repudiated them. The mammy, the tragic mulatta, and the jezebel or sexual black woman have all appeared on the American stage in both mainstream and African American dramas during the nineteenth and twentieth centuries. The mammy and the mulatta have been represented both positively and negatively, whereas the jezebel remains primarily the domain of the dominant culture (although she occasionally appears in dramas by African American men), and any positive transformation of this particular character requires a reenvisioning of black women's sexuality.

The African American women playwrights included here were

4

committed to "advancing the race," to use an early twentieth-century trope. They have attempted to change the dominant culture's ideas about blacks and about black identity by creating drama that better represented the issues, concerns, and lives of African Americans. They also have created positive images for blacks in which they could see their own lives. In this, they follow a long tradition of "race women" from the nineteenth century who advocated rights and recognition for all African Americans. While they addressed representation of blacks by the dominant culture, until recently the plays written by these women were largely performed for audiences within the black community, when they were performed at all. Many were published, especially during the early part of the century, in periodicals such as *Crisis* and *Opportunity*, and some were gathered into anthologies.

In the theatre, we often think of the stage as a mirror, one that reflects the reality of our lives and shows that reality to us. We particularly think of modern realism in this way. However, the stage can sometimes be more like a funnyhouse mirror, to use Adrienne Kennedy's powerful image (1964), which does not show our reality as it is, but as it is perceived through the eyes of others. As the audience views the performance and actors, the images shown on stage are colored by the audience's experience, the actors' previous and present performances, and the director's staging. While most play scripts are the work of a single vision, those same scripts put on stage become the "reality" of the plays as seen through the eyes of those who have worked to produce it. Instead of the stage giving us an objective reflection, it always gives us a very subjective representation. The stage images can, inadvertently, become icons.

"Daddy" Rice's Jim Crow minstrel figure is one example of this kind of distorted reflection. Examining this figure of an old black man reveals the process of iconization. White minstrel performers selectively chose dances, songs, and traditions of slaves, exaggerated what they saw as comic elements, and presented them as a true representation of blacks. It was a lucrative business, as minstrel shows were extremely popular. The audiences, especially those who had little or no contact with Southern blacks, believed that the minstrel figures were accurate representations. The figures then replaced real Southern blacks in the popular imagination; the "real" became the minstrel character, and thus the icon of Jim Crow replaced the real black man whom Rice had observed. The minstrel shows helped create stereotypes of African Americans. Many minstrel shows toured Northern cities and were popular with working-class immigrants, who were reassured by the existence of a group that had lower socioeconomic status than they. Two African American women characters were created—the mammy and the mulatta. The mammy figure, performed by white men, was ignorant and spoke in malapropisms, much like her black male counterparts. She was portrayed as large, happy, and aggressively or even animalistically sexual. As with other black minstrel figures, her markers of blackness—eyes, nose, and lips particularly—were exaggerated. The mulatta, on the other hand, because of her "white blood," was thinner, wore more refined clothes, and had less exaggerated features than the mammy. She was however still tainted, and although she spoke English more properly, she was a coquettish character who inevitably possessed some tragic flaw that would lead to her downfall.

These two characters, so firmly established in the nineteenth century, were eventually joined by the jezebel after the turn of the century. The post-Civil War mammy evolved into the neutered house servant, and the sexually promiscuous black woman was confined to the jezebel type.

There was another force that emerged in the twentieth century, which generated new and different representations of African Americans: the emergent black middle class focused much of its energy on creating art. Their primary encouragement came in the person of W. E. B. Du Bois. Instead of the stereotyped characters of the mammy and the mulatta, playwrights Georgia Douglas Johnson, May Miller, Marita Bonner, Eulalie Spence, and Zora Neale Hurston, among others, delved into the lives of African Americans as they were lived. Du Bois noted:

The white public today demands from its artists, literary and pictorial, race pre-judgement which deliberately distorts Truth and Justice, as far as colored races are concerned, and it will pay for no other. On the other hand, the young and slowly growing black public still wants its prophets almost equally unfree. We are bound by all sorts of customs that have come down as second-hand clothes of white patrons. We are ashamed of sex and we lower our eyes when people will talk of it. (1971: 320)

Du Bois, as this commentary indicates, was most interested in putting forth images that presented blacks' lives as they were lived—in a word, "Truth."

Yet even these representations were not completely the "Truth." In their fervor to prove both that the images created by whites were inaccurate and that blacks were morally equal to whites, some middle-class African American artists excluded lower-class blacks from their representations. These representations had to show not only the hardship, but also the courage, determination, and virtuous lives of blacks. Du Bois's counsel to show the breadth of black experience was not fully realized until the 1960s.

The slow development of positive representations of black sexuality is a function of middle-class values and the resistance to the myth of an immoral black sexuality. The myth of the rapacious black man haunted the lives of thousands of blacks, particularly in the South. Tales of black men raping white women resulted in lynch mobs who, in their murderous frenzy, would kill the first black they could find. Black women were powerless against the mobs that entered their homes and forcibly removed their husbands, sons, and fathers; if the accused men weren't home, the women of the household would likely be raped, or lynched, or both. When the women were raped, another aspect of the myth was invoked; as historian Gerda Lerner states, "A myth was created that all black women were eager for sexual exploits, voluntarily 'loose'

7

in their morals and, therefore, deserved none of the consideration and respect granted to white women. Every black woman was, by definition, a slut" (1972: 163). The myth was convenient for the white men who desired black women; indeed, it was a projection of this desire. The mythic perception also dehumanized blacks, for they were believed unable to control their sexuality, which made them closer to animals.

Class and education could not shield blacks; as Paula Giddings notes, "The stereotype of Black women, like that of Black men, applied to all classes, including the middle-class leaders"(1984: 83). Black women who were raped had little or no legal recourse, unlike white women, who, while they may not have had legal recourse themselves, had white men to punish black offenders. Many of the women playwrights of the Harlem Renaissance would deal with the issue of miscegenation in their plays, not out of opposition to the mixing of races, but in response to the reality of the widespread situation of white men's sexual license over black women. As Angela Davis points out in her book *Women, Race and Class* (1983), the children of miscegenation were often not children of love, but children of rape; it is also noted by Franz Fanon in *Black Skins, White Masks* (1952). These children were usually not acknowledged by their white fathers; however, they were generally accepted into the black community.

Out of these social and economic circumstances came black playwrights and filmmakers whose task was and continues to be a difficult one; through their dramas and films, they are charged with opposing the iconic representations of black men and women that have existed since the days of legalized slavery. The dominant icons, while specifically part of cultural or aesthetic production, maintain the supremacy of whites. Our examination of dramatic and filmic productions by African American women will show how these women resist the dominant icons and present alternatives to them. In doing so, they provide us with the cultural resources that help us to resist and dismantle structures and imagery that assault and deny our lives meaning.

8

Chapter 1

Mama on the Couch?

The icon of the mammy is probably the most recognizable and longest perpetuated image of African American women in American society, and it has been reproduced again and again on stage and screen. If there were any doubt about its pervasiveness, a look at black women presented on many television sitcoms will reveal her continued presence. The disdain in which African Americans hold this image is nearly as strong; one need only look at *The Colored Museum* (1986). George C. Wolfe's play includes a mammy, or, as he portrays her, Mama on the Couch, in his satire on African American images in theatre. Wolfe's depiction is associated with the domineering woman who tries to control the lives of those around her, and specifically alludes to Lorraine Hansberry's character Lena Younger from *A Raisin in the Sun* (1959). But whose mammy is she? Is she really Hansberry's Mama? Is there a difference between the origin of mammy and that of Mama Younger? We will explore the myth and reality of this character, and the contrasting representations of mothering. As will be shown, there is a substantial difference between the mammy characters of the white imagination, from which Wolfe actually derives his Mama, and the mother characters in the plays written by black women, the tradition out of which Lena Younger was created. Mothers and mammies on stage and screen are examined here in three time periods: 1915 to 1919, 1925 to 1940, and 1957 to 1960.

9

Yes Ma'am, Miss Scarlett

The mammy is descended from a white image of the slave woman, and she first appears in the minstrel show. As the "Negro wench" (Isaacs 1947: 25), she is typified visually by the kerchief tied around her head, her apron, and her large size, as well as her racial markers of big lips and a wide nose. This figure is modified and dignified in white-constructed images in later years, but semiotically she remains the same. Her position is still defined by her race; any upward mobility is restricted by her skin color. Like the black men presented in the minstrel show, the original "Negro wench" is an ignorant slave whose speech is filled with malapropisms.

The mammy is also the symbol of black motherhood as perceived by whites. In the mythic construction, the black woman "mammy" is the caretaker of the whites' homes and children first, and her own second. Her primary duties are to the whites for whom she works. She must sacrifice the needs of her own family for those of the white family that employs her. Usually she is not shown to have a family of her own at all. The picture of her existing without a family of her own accentuates her status as property, as the children of a slave would have been the master's property. Toni Morrison's description of the characterization of Jim (in *Huck Finn*) can be extended to describe this icon of black women—mammies—in the white imagination: "[there is an] apparently limitless store of love and compassion the black [woman] has for [her] white friend and white masters; and [her] assumption that the whites are indeed what they say they are, superior and adult" (1992: 56). In essence, then, the mammy is a black woman who focuses her time, love, devotion, and attention on whites, particularly her "adopted" white family, rather than on her own black family.

There were, of course, historical black women who worked as domestics. This work enabled them to help feed their families and supplement or replace the incomes of their husbands, who might not have been able to find work or were only able to find occasional work. The mammy's work was rooted in historical fact, even if other elements of the icon are a departure from historical reality. As Margaret Wilkerson states, she was the "neutered, domineering mammy who ruled the roost" (1986: xiv). Part of the slave woman's labor had been reproduction, but rather than reproducing human beings for their own sake, she produced them as capital for her master. Like the animals owned by the master, she was partnered with the male most likely to produce the most valuable offspring. The black woman's procreation duties were divorced from sexual pleasure.

As a fictional mammy for white children, she is not an authentic mother; in other words, her "mothering" is not connected to the biological process of giving birth. Thus the mammy's sexuality is separate from her motherhood, and the children for whom she cares are not her own. Her position is devoid of the power that would be hers if she were the biological mother of the children for whom she cares.

The image of the neutered mammy appears in one of the earliest American films, D. W. Griffith's *The Birth of a Nation* (1915), which was the first widely disseminated visual representation of blacks. Griffith unconvincingly disclaims his representation, implying that he is alternately creating fiction or representing history. Based on *The Clansman*, a novel by the Reverend Thomas Dixon, the project of this film was to present the Southern aristocracy as sympathetic and tragic in the period immediately following the Civil War. According to the film, white Southern citizens must face aggression and dominance by ignorant blacks, and they are justified in developing the Ku Klux Klan to maintain order. The mammy isn't even granted a name; she is still only a slave, after all, and doesn't need one. The white actress who plays her is obviously in blackface makeup to accentuate those identifying lips and eyes; she is large, dressed in her standard slave wear, including apron and kerchief. She pursues her duties with all the fervor of the good slave who is grateful to the family that owns her. The mammy cares for the youngest Cameron sister, loving her as if she were her own child. She isn't shown as having any children of her own.

Throughout the film, she displays behavior characteristic of a mammy, that is, a "good" Negro. In one scene, renegade Union soldiers attack the Cameron house. The Cameron women hide in the basement, and the mammy disappears to some safe place. Confederates come to their rescue in the nick of time, just after the Union soldiers have set fire to the house. Mammy appears and hugs a Confederate soldier to thank him for saving her from the evil Northern blacks. The Confederate soldiers' act maintains their hierarchical relationship with blacks. As Gayatri Spivak describes in her article "Can the Subaltern Speak?" their behavior expresses the phenomenon of "white men saving brown women from brown men" (Nelson and Grossberg 1988: 297). In *The Birth of a Nation*, the colonizer/master takes it upon himself to demonstrate his patriarchal concern for the colonized/enslaved by protecting mammy (good) from men of her own race (bad) who, in this case, were fighting for her freedom as well as their own. This action reinforces the mythic dominance of whites and the acceptance of it by "good" blacks, especially the mammy.

After the Civil War, Griffith's mammy rules the old roost, staying with her master's family out of love and duty. When Stillwell, the patriarch of the Northern family arrives, he brings his black servant. Mammy is appalled at the servant's haughty behavior. He begins to hand her his master's bags, and she is offended. In this Southern social order, it is his responsibility to carry out his own duties. She remarks after an exchange with him, "Dem free niggers from de North is crazy!" Since she is content in her life as a slave, she feels that she owes her allegiance to the people who owned her. She never makes decisions; she is there to support the decisions of the master. Her self-sacrifice and loyalty are evident. She is even responsible for rescuing the colonel from a black mob after he has been arrested for the murder of Lynch, the powerful mulatto in league with the carpetbaggers. Semiotically, the mammy is presented as black, despite the fact that she is played by a white woman in blackface. Not only does her blackface makeup accentuate the actress's second role as presenter, but it also emphasizes to a contemporary audience that the mammy is a white representation of blackness.

To be sure, the film repeatedly asserts its fictionality. Griffith uses storyboards that frequently claim he is not representing real people or events, but it is difficult to accept the film as fiction. He undermines his claim of fictionality with other storyboards within the film that claim he is creating "historic reconstructions" of events. By mixing the fiction of the "little Colonel's" family with the reality of the Civil War and Reconstruction periods, Griffith makes it difficult to discern which are depictions of real events and which are fictionalized. For example, popular knowledge of the Ku Klux Klan places its origins in the South during Reconstruction, as Griffith's film presents; in actuality, the Klan emerged in the Midwest (Indiana or Tennessee, depending on the source).

Also, it cannot be ignored that the viewing of the film had very real effects on the population. Aside from invigorating and enriching the motion picture industry, its outrageous and blatantly racist stereotypes of blacks and glorification of the Ku Klux Klan mobilized blacks, especially the NAACP, to fight against such representations. Years before, the play adapted from Dixon's book had caused riots at its staging in Philadelphia. Thomas Cripps in his *Slow Fade to Black* (1993b: 67) asserts that the NAACP's protests against the film helped to secure its position as an "icon of racism worshipped by racists largely because of the reputation given it by the NAACP." Because the NAACP so despised the film, racists embraced it as the ultimate proof of the legitimacy of racism. The film swelled the ranks of the Ku Klux Klan; the number of lynchings in the South increased at a time when blacks were trying to vote and protesting against unfair work practices, and black women were being educated in greater numbers. The images in this film are so disgusting and outrageous that it is difficult to sit through the two videotapes available for private viewing.

The icon of the mammy was alive and well in the white imagination as the century continued. In the 1930s, three popular mammies appeared in dramatic works and fiction by white women: Addie in Lillian Hellman's play *The Little Foxes*, Mammy in the filmed version of Margaret Mitchell's novel *Gone With the Wind*, and Delilah in the first film adaptation of Fannie Hurst's novel *Imitation of Life*.

Abbie Mitchell's role as Addie in Hellman's 1939 play *The Little Foxes* replicates many of the same visual and cultural representations of black women that are found in Griffith's film. The black characters in the play are committed to maintaining the well-being of the family they serve. Addie is the first person seen on stage, performing her duties of keeping the house in order and watching to make sure that Cal, the black male servant, does as he is told. In these first few moments of the play, we see evidence of her devotion to the family and particularly to Alexandra (Zan), the young woman she has taken care of for many years. Addie's devotion to Zan is evidenced further when Addie volunteers to go to Baltimore with seventeen-year-old Zan on the journey to bring her ailing father, Horace, back home.

Addie, it would seem, has no life except the one she lives in the Giddens's home. Addie functions as a substitute mother for Zan, playing the neuter yet maternal figure so long associated with the mammy. Zan bypasses her own mother, Regina, and asks Addie if she can have a glass of port at the beginning of the play. Addie, played by black actress Abbie Mitchell, is much more involved in the events of the family's lives, and much more dignified than her predecessor in *The Birth of a Nation*. Her speech is more refined, and she is not treated as a child. The play is set in 1900, which could account for the increase in dignity allowed the mammy. She is no longer a slave, but an employee, and as a result is deserving of more respect than a slave. Addie takes it upon herself to care for Horace and Alexandra as a guardian and a nurturer. Hellman manages to avoid romanticizing the Old South, and shows instead the corruption beneath the veneer of respectability. In addition to her care for Zan, Addie demonstrates her devotion by informing Horace about the "deal" struck between Regina and Oscar, her brother, which promises Alexandra to her first cousin Leo. When Horace's health diminishes, Addie nurses him. Addie takes on a motherly role for her surrogate family. By siding with Horace and Zan against the machinations of Regina and Oscar, Addie also is keeper of the moral order, an asexual guardian. Addie fits the mammy's role in all ways: she guards and protects white womanhood, is employed as a servant, is a moral influence, has no black family, and works to maintain white supremacy.

The film *Gone With the Wind* (1939) is much more blatant than Hellman's play in its recalling of the grand old days of Southern aristocracy, including the happy, obedient slaves who were, and yet were not, part of the family. It was not without controversy; many blacks were opposed to the making of the film, and they persuaded David O. Selznick to remove the word "nigger" from the script and to exclude references to the Ku Klux Klan. With its Civil War and Glory of the South themes, it recalled Griffith's film for many viewers; there are even scenes in *Gone With the Wind* that look much like scenes from *The Birth of a Nation*. According to the documentary on the making of *Gone With the Wind*, blacks "accepted their roles in a climate of disapproval." Black critics and actors felt that the roles were demeaning. However, some good came of the film for blacks in Hollywood; Hattie McDaniel won an Oscar for her performance, the first black to do so. In her acceptance speech, she expressed the hope that her winning would prove the competency of her people and open more opportunities to them.

According to *The Making of a Legend: Gone With the Wind* (1989), the documentary produced by Selznick's son, Selznick was sympathetic about material "which [blacks] regarded as insulting and damaging." David O. Selznick claimed that his sympathy for European Jews, persecuted by Adolf Hitler, influenced his decision to edit the script. Selznick made connections between the negative portrayals of Jews in Nazi propaganda and negative portrayals of blacks in American media. For all of his effort, blacks were still

displeased with the film, including those who had roles in it. Butter-
fly McQueen, who played Prissy, remarked in her interview in the
documentary:

> I hated the part then; Mr. Selznick understood that it was a
> difficult part for an intelligent person to play, 'cause it was
> 1938, and I didn't think anybody would go back and have me
> to be a little slave, but I did everything they asked me except I
> wouldn't let them slap me and I wouldn't eat the watermelon.
> Mammy [Hattie McDaniel] said, You'll never come back to
> Hollywood, you complain too much.

Despite the script changes Selznick's film retains the stereotypes of
the original novel.

The mammy of this film is even named Mammy. She functions
as Scarlett's surrogate mother and protector. Even while Scarlett's
mother is alive, Mammy is the one in whom Scarlett confides. Scarlett's mother seems unaware of her daughter's love for Ashley
Wilkes, while Mammy is not only aware but also seeks to protect
Scarlett from her own stubborn infatuation. Mammy occasionally
seems helpless to intervene against the machinations of Scarlett
because of her position as a servant. This class difference creates
additional tension in their relationship that is not evident in Zan's
relationship with Addie. There is an element of reverence for
Mammy, especially on the part of Scarlett, who at times treats her
as a mother (she has, after all, raised Scarlett), and yet, at the same
time regards Mammy as an "inferior."

Mammy's pride is rooted in her indispensability to the O'Hara
family. She beams to Melanie after the birth of Scarlett's daughter,
"This sho' is a happy day. I done diapered three generations of this
family." When Scarlett's mother dies, Mammy doesn't replace her,
but instead becomes an assistant to Scarlett in running the house.
The motherless household is desperate; during the time when there
is no patriarchal head of the household, Scarlett marries her sister's
fiancé, is nearly raped, and causes her husband's death. When

there is a man as the head of the household, particularly in the character of Rhett Butler, order is maintained or restored and events tend to unfold positively. The lack of a mother makes the white patriarch more important.

Mammy still has a great deal of authority among the slaves and with the family. Unlike the mammy in Griffith's movie, Mammy has become the all-knowing and interfering (with good intentions) guardian of the family. She is also appointed (or takes upon herself) the role of defender of white womanhood, especially that of the Southern lady. She admonishes Scarlett on several occasions to not "act like poor white trash children," and attempts to ensure that Scarlett presents herself as a lady at all times.

There are some thematic similarities to Griffith's film in addition to the visual ones, despite Cripps's assertion in *Slow Fade to Black* that the film "calculatedly enlarged and humanized traditional black roles" (1993b: 362n). There are advances in Mammy, but she remains the neutered, domineering presence that was presented in Griffith's film. There is no explanation for why Mammy stays with Scarlett after she has been freed; her freedom is never mentioned or questioned. Mammy even pushes aside a group of freedmen who are dancing on the streets of Reconstruction Atlanta so that Scarlett doesn't have to walk around them. Mammy not only controls and disperses the black men, but protects and honors her white mistress. We also never see Mammy being paid for her services; they are simply expected. Thus *Gone With the Wind* shares a reverence for the old Southern way of life with *The Birth of a Nation*, but it does not have the overtly hateful and intentionally deceitful depictions of renegade black soldiers wreaking havoc on the South; instead, the "real enemy" is a detail of white Union soldiers. This is one of Selznick's adjustments. Rather than have Scarlett attacked by black soldiers, they are white; she is instead helped by a black man. The mob that her husband forms is, therefore, not a group of Klansmen.

Yet another screen mammy appeared in the 1930s: Aunt Delilah in the original version of *Imitation of Life*, in 1934. The film is

based on Fannie Hurst's novel of the same name. Aunt Delilah joins
with Miss Bea, a white woman, and the two widows try to make a
go of it in the world. They struggle during the Depression until Miss
Bea decides to market Delilah's pancake mix, handed down in the
family for generations. Miss Bea offers Delilah a share, but Delilah
refuses, claiming that she wants to remain with the family as a
servant. Delilah, played by Louise Beavers, is a physically smaller
version of Hattie McDaniel; Beavers and McDaniel played the majority of mammy roles in Hollywood during the 1930s. Delilah,
Bea, and their daughters live happily for years, until problems surface with their daughters. Delilah's daughter, Peola, very light-
skinned, is determined to pass for white. Miss Bea's daughter, Jessie, becomes her mother's rival in love. Interestingly, the parentage
of both daughters is left ambiguous; in a sense, they have the same
absent white father, still determining their lives. Aunt Delilah's
elaborate funeral ends the film. Unfortunately, this early version of
the film is not readily available.

While much of the film is rooted in solid stereotypes, it also
defies some of them. The women are able to become financially
stable without having a man in the house. Delilah's pancake mix
ensures their success, but it is ultimately a joint effort. Peola was
actually played by a black woman, Fredi Washington, who would
be the last black woman to play a film mulatta in a mainstream
film until recently. Washington had difficulty being cast in film
roles, and her "type" was only discovered when she played with
Paul Robeson in *Black Boy*.

The 1950s were much more conservative in many ways. *Imitation of Life* was remade with some substantial differences in
1959, the same year Lorraine Hansberry's *A Raisin in the Sun* appeared on Broadway; the 1959 version is an imitation of an imitation of life, a double visual mimesis. As an imitation of an
imitation, it is even further removed from the realm of the real
(Fannie Hurst's novel was, of course, the "original" imitation).

In the 1959 version of the film, the widows are Lora and
Annie. Annie, the black woman (whose name sounds similar to

mammy), finds Lora's young daughter, Susie, on the beach. Annie convinces Lora, played by Lana Turner, to take her and her white-looking daughter, Sarah Jane, back to the city with them. Annie quickly makes herself indispensable around the house, while Lora attempts to make an acting career for herself. As in the early version, they struggle until the miracle comes to save them from poverty. However, it is not Annie who is responsible for the bit of fortune that saves the family, but Lora. Lora lands an acting role, and her career takes off from there. Annie minds the house, and Lora goes on to fame and fortune, always keeping Annie and Sarah Jane with her, reasserting a patriarchal model with Lora as the money-earning father figure. In contrast to the first version of this film, Annie never once makes a pancake, although she physically is much like Delilah.

The relationship between the two women, from this point on in the film, closely parallels the original film. Annie takes care of Lora and her daughter dutifully through their good years. The later years are free from financial problems, but marked by personal ones. Again, the difficulties are Sarah Jane's desire to pass for white, which has plagued her all of her years, and Susie's adolescent crush on her mother's lover, Steve. Another lavish funeral concludes the film, demonstrating Annie's importance within her own community and the respect she has there. The prodigal Sarah Jane returns and throws herself melodramatically on her mother's coffin.

There are occasions where the distance between Lora and Annie is accentuated. After they have become successful, Annie speaks to Lora about plans for her funeral. Annie mentions that she wants all of her friends present, and Lora responds with surprise; she didn't realize that Annie had any life at all outside the family. Of course, we are treated to a church overflowing with people at Annie's funeral. This moment shows unusual insight into the relationship between mistress and servant, acknowledging Annie's life outside the home in which she works, as well as Lora's ignorance of it. The other improvement of the mammy's image is the inclusion of Annie's own family. This change is one that will make its way into other mammy characters. Unfortunately, it doesn't make up for the remainder of the film, nor for Annie's steadfast and incredible insistence on maintaining her proper subordinate place, and encouraging her daughter to do the same.

The melodramatic scene of Annie's death is accentuated by Lora's extreme reactions. They are entirely self-centered; she does not want Annie to leave her. The tension between the master and the servant rises, as was seen between Scarlett and Mammy in *Gone With the Wind*. Lora feels that she is closer to Annie than she actually is; Lora demonstrates a familiarity usually reserved for one's own family. After spending years living and working with Lora, Annie feels a sense of duty and connection. She has always nurtured all three of the white (or white-looking) women in her care, and has also mothered them. Annie is still responsible for guarding white womanhood, and while Lora actively pursues two relationships during the course of the film, Annie essentially remains the neutered caretaker. The audience doesn't see Annie involved with men; indeed, she is the only one of the four who does not have a physical or emotional relationship with a man during the film. We know that Annie had one sexual relationship, and that with a white-looking (if not in fact white) man. It becomes impossible to show Annie with a white man because it is taboo; likewise, it is impossible to show her with a black man because of the inherent sexuality that the two of them would symbolize. Annie, as a mother figure, cannot simultaneously embody sexuality and motherhood; the black woman who is permitted sexuality must be a prostitute (cf. chapter 3). Annie guards white womanhood against trespasses, even when the transgressor is her own daughter.

Even on her deathbed, she refers to Lora as "Miss Lora," in an echo of "Miss Scarlett," which exposes the reality of their relationship despite all of Lora's attempts to make them friends rather than employer and employee. Annie's efforts have ensured the success of herself, Lora, and their daughters. She managed the money for the four of them, keeping them from starvation and homelessness, but she has also succeeded in shoring up the status quo: white supremacy.

The mammy image also appears in both the stage production and the film version of Carson McCullers's *The Member of the Wedding*, which premiered in 1951. The visual image is familiar: that of a large black woman, this time with a hat instead of a bandanna and apron. Berenice's primary concern is the welfare of the young white children in her care, reproducing the relationship of Mammy in *Gone With the Wind*; McCullers shares the white Southern female experience with Mitchell. Berenice seems to exist as though she has no life outside the family for which she works, like Mitchell's Mammy. Yet in a departure from the earlier roles, and like Annie in *Imitation of Life*, this mammy does have her own family. Her family is not only mentioned in the play but also is physically present. Her son, Honey, stays in trouble for challenging whites as Sarah Jane does, albeit in different ways. Despite Honey's presence, Berenice is still the quintessential mammy. She is a surrogate mother for the children, although John Henry's mother is still alive and present to care for him. Like Scarlett O'Hara, Frankie is brought up by her mammy, Berenice. Berenice seems powerless to effect any change at all; she is not even responsible for Frankie's personal growth (or lack thereof) by the end of the play. Berenice is unable to save either of her "sons," John Henry or Honey. Her only act of independence is resigning when the family decides to move. As in both versions of *Imitation of Life*, the problems within the mammy's own biological family stem from uppity children who refuse to do as their mothers did and accept their servile role with a smile.

Both Honey and John Henry die before the end of the play. Honey is imprisoned after knifing a white man in the town and allegedly hangs himself in jail; John Henry dies of meningitis. Because the cards are stacked against Honey, it seems that there is greater tragedy in John Henry's death. Berenice says, reminiscing about the week that both of them died, "Honey gone and John Henry, my little boy, gone" (McCullers 1951: 114). Honey was her son, in fact, "all the family [she's] got" (94). She seems more concerned and saddened over the death of John Henry, who did not deserve to die. Honey, on the other hand, had flaunted the authority of the white men in the town, which made his life forfeit and his death deserved. John Henry was a child, and because he was white and innocent, could not ever be guilty of the same insolence.

In this play, which is allegedly about the growing pains of a young white woman, the central character is Berenice. Frankie changes very little, and even the three monumental events in her life (her brother's marriage, her cousin's death, and Honey's death) do not affect her. Berenice is the first and last character we see on stage, and while only minimally affected by the wedding, she is the most changed character by the end of the play. She is strangely saddened by the changes. Her losses have created a completely new reality for her. Instead of caring for Frankie, she is now "free." She cannot see the benefit in her own "freedom," which is accompanied by the deaths of her "boys." In light of the changes that were emerging in the early 1950s in terms of civil rights, her sadness about her freedom is suspect. Then again, as a mammy, Berenice could hardly be interested in any liberatory movement. The conservatism she demonstrates with Honey is in line with the type of matriarch that Daniel Patrick Moynihan would create more than a decade later.

In the American imagination, the mammy is one representation of black women. This icon had many of the same elements as what would come to be known as the black matriarch. The icon, present in stage and film, has become familiar to the American public. Because of her presence in films like *Gone With the Wind*, and in characters like Aunt Jemima, the mammy was disdained in the middle-class black community. She was viewed not only as a negative stereotype, but also as harmful to the efforts of black women in their communities and in the society as a whole. This maternal slave figure was associated with the repression of the black man.

In the mid-1960s, Moynihan wrote his famous report that connected the fictional screen mammy with real black women. Moynihan's characterizations of black women as matriarchs and emasculators in league with white men influenced the black men who were coming to power. Moynihan's report played on the black and white patriarchal fears of the nascent women's movement. After studying U.S. census reports from 1960 and data from Harlem Youth Opportunities Unlimited, Inc., Moynihan wrote that "the cause of ghetto problems [was] in the [nature of the] Negro family and not in unemployment or any of the other institutional sources of deprivation (Moynihan in Rainwater and Yancy 1967: 142). There was "evidence," from nearly a century of images from stage and screen, that confirmed Moynihan's assertions. The matriarch described in the report recalled these old white stereotypes of black women. The mammy became the matriarch incarnate, invoking images of McDaniel and Beavers. Black women's work outside the home, previously valued as a contribution to the household, allegedly eroded the black man's sense of manhood. Any images of black women that contradicted those perpetuated by the dominant culture were obscured, if not silenced; some of them had been lost over the years. However, black women did not simply accept these images from the white imaginations. Since the early years of the twentieth century, black women had been working to counteract and diversify the representations of themselves.

Alternative Nurture

The realities of the lives of black women were, of course, only remotely like the images of them on the stage and screen. African American women playwrights took up W. E. B. Du Bois's challenge to revolutionize their portrayal on the stage. The first of the plays to present different black women on stage was Angelina Weld Grimke's *Rachel*. Grimke's play has no mammies at all. Instead, the two primary women characters of the play, Rachel and her mother, give a substantially different portrait of the lives of black women, who are sometimes mothers, and who must sometimes care for their families alone, but whose vision of nurturing does not include caring for white families.

According to Carolyn Stubbs (1978), Grimke wrote her play in response to *The Birth of a Nation*, which premiered in 1915. Grimke's work was in direct response to the film's negative images of blacks, including black women. It was performed in March 1916; a note in the program states that "this is the first attempt to use the stage for race propaganda in order to enlighten the American people relative to the lamentable condition of ten millions of colored citizens in this free Republic." The committee (which included Anna Julia Cooper and Archibald Grimke), playwright, and director, Nathaniel Guy, were very much aware of the use of this play. It also stands as a theatrical monument, in contrast to the bronze "Black Mammies" monument that had been proposed by the Daughters of the Confederacy. The Daughters of the Confederacy proposed that a statue be erected to honor the black women who had fulfilled their roles as mammies for them. At the time, Chandler Owen, coeditor of the Washington, D.C., black paper *The Messenger*, proposed a

> monument to the Negro women who have risen above insult, assault, debauchery, prostitution, and abuse *to which these unfortunate "black mammies" were subjected.* . . . Let this "mammy" statue go. Let it fade away. . . . Let [a different statue's] white shaft point like a lofty mountain peak to a *New Negro Mother,* no longer a *"white man's woman,"* no longer the sex-enslaved *"black mammy"* of Dixie—but the apotheosis of triumphant Negro womanhood. (Quoted in Giddings 1984: 184)

Grimke's play could function as that monument.

Rachel's mother works as a seamstress, not as a domestic in anyone's house. She is a single mother, not because of moral laxity, but because her husband was lynched. She is not domineering, and supports her children both emotionally and financially. Her husband and one son were lynched when the paper her husband owned and edited protested the lynching of another innocent black man. Rachel does have maternal tendencies; she is like the original folk persona Aunt Jemima, who loved and was loved by children. Beverly Johnson has found in her research on the Aunt Jemima figure and the actress Edith Goodall Wilson that the figure dates to the mid-nineteenth century, long before the mammy figure who was appropriated to sell pancake batter for Quaker Oats. As Johnson explains, the name Jemima means "she who comes in peace," and that "Aunt" in this case should be interpreted in the black community/extended family sense, rather than in the sense of whites who called servants and wet nurses "auntie." Johnson found an historical figure who took care of the community's black children during the Civil War, while others were off fighting in the war.

In the first scene of Grimke's play, we are treated to a vision of Rachel glowing over a young boy who lives in the apartment below hers. Her mother says, "You're not happy unless some child is trailing along in your rear" (Hatch and Shine 1974: 140). Rachel loves the black children in her neighborhood as though they were her own. Her enthusiasm for children is curbed when her mother finally tells her of the fate of her half-brother and father. "Why—it would be more merciful—to strangle the little things at birth. And so this nation—this white Christian nation—has deliberately set its curse upon the most beautiful—the most holy thing in life— motherhood!" (149).

Rachel's sentiment is not unfounded, nor is it unrealistic. In fact, there were women who killed their children rather than see them grow up in a system that was set against them. It is a kind of nurture different from that of the mammy who only supports; this nurture is one that understands the circumstances of life and limited possibilities. There are accounts in slave narratives of women who would prefer to see their children dead than to have them grow up in slavery. Slavery meant that in all likelihood, mothers would be separated from their children when either they or their children were sold. As recounted in one slave narrative:

> Thus my mother and father were hired to Tennessee. The next morning they were to leave. I saw ma working around with the baby under her arms as if it had been a bundle of some kind. Pa came up to the cabin with an old mare for ma to ride, and an old mule for himself. Mr. Jennings was with him.
>
> "Fannie, leave the baby with Aunt Mary," said Mr. Jennings very quietly. At this, ma took the baby by its feet, a foot in each hand, and with the baby's head swinging downward, she vowed to smash its brains out before she'd leave it. . . . Ma took her baby with her. (quoted in Lerner 1972: 38)

There were other instances of women carrying out such threats to prevent their children from being sold from them, and to ensure that their female children would not have to grow up to become breeders for white masters. Black women also used herbs to bring on miscarriages, depriving their masters of children as property to be bought and sold (Gutman 1976: 80n–82n).

Rachel, much like this slave woman, loses her faith in a just system. Her dream of having children is gone, and instead she says that "no child of mine shall ever lie upon my breast, for I will not have it rise up, in the terrible days that are to be—and call me cursed" (Hatch and Shine 1974: 161). She vows that, like God, she chooses to kill, but as she says, "I kill at once—I do not torture" (161). Although many thought that Grimke advanced Rachel's speeches and actions, Grimke rejects the notion that she was advocating genocide. Instead, she is calling attention to the dilemma facing blacks during the period. She wanted to confront the images and beliefs of whites, who thought "that all colored people are a grinning, white-toothed, shiftless, carefree set, given to chicken-stealing, watermelon-eating, always, under all circumstances, properly obsequious to a white skin" (quoted in Stubbs 1978: 147).

The early twentieth century was not a good time for blacks. "By 1918 the cost-of-living index had risen 69 percent above the level of just four years earlier, while wages were going down" (Giddings 1984: 139). Many blacks in the South were jailed and used as a pool for free labor. The practice consisted of arresting blacks, particularly black men, on trumped-up charges; anyone who was jailed could be forced to work. Because of the increased economic difficulties in the South, many blacks were moving North in hopes of better opportunity. Their situation was somewhat better there; women could earn much more in the North, even as domestics. Positions as clerks and secretaries opened up for black women when white women were promoted or took higher-paying jobs. As Grimke shows in her play, however, the opportunities that opened up for black women were not unbounded.

Unlike the images perpetuated by Griffith's film, black women of the 1910s, especially those of the middle class, were increasingly better educated. To compete with white women, black women had to have more education. While some had children, the leaders of the period were more focused on the welfare of the race as a whole. Dozens of black women's clubs were formed in the late nineteenth century, and they continued into the twentieth. Their concept of nurturing was to care for the race, to "lift as we climb," to quote the motto of the National Association of Colored Women. Like the middle-class black women of her time, Grimke's Rachel is educated, attempts to help out the children of her neighborhood, and wishes to become a teacher. Grimke's portrayal of Rachel honors the women who contributed so much to their race: they supported suffrage, opposed lynching, started unions and colleges, and provided assistance for young women who went north looking for opportunity.

Rachel's employment aspirations are never achieved, as there are no teaching positions available for her. She has resigned herself to a life devoid of that which would fulfill her most. When John Strong asks if she has heard anything about her applications, she replies, "No, nor ever will be [anything encouraging from the schools]. I know that now. There's no more chance for me than there is for Tom,—or than there was for you—or for any of us with dark skins. It's lucky for me that I love to keep house, and cook, and sew. I'll never get anything else"(Hatch and Shine 1974: 156). But unlike the mammies of the screen, Rachel will not conform to the expectations of whites; the children she will value and nurture are those of her own community. In the increasing desolation of the family, she makes the agonizing choice to kill the young man she has adopted, because she cannot see a decent life for him, even as an educated black man, beyond employment as a waiter or porter.

By the 1930s, the situation wasn't much better for blacks than it had been in the 1910s. Blacks were the hardest hit by the Depression, but black women seemed to be doing better economically than black men. "By 1930 four out of every ten graduates from Black colleges were women and their numbers were increasing" (Giddings 1984: 205). Unfortunately, this still did not ensure that black women's lives were better. They felt the Depression more acutely than white women did; in New York City, domestic workers would line up "on empty lots in the Bronx each day, regardless of the weather, to wait for prospective employers who bargained for their day's services" (204). Those services might include their bodies.

There was also a dramatic rise in lynchings during the early years of the Depression. Desperate economic conditions contributed to the interracial tension that already existed, and white men who felt threatened by black men exercised their power by attacking them.

In 1935, W. E. B. Du Bois began to advocate the strengthening of black institutions, rather than the integration of white ones. To Du Bois, "integration for its own sake was both meaningless and demeaning," as Giddings interprets his views (1984: 211). The late 1920s and early 1930s had produced a growing body of dramatic literature by African Americans that reflected a variety of viewpoints, including those espoused by Du Bois. During the Harlem Renaissance, there were no fewer than thirty black women who tried their hand at writing drama. Some wrote about the "folk," setting their plays in the South in the late nineteenth and early twentieth centuries, while others wrote historical pageants about black historical figures and plays of Northern urban life.

Following in the footsteps of Angelina Weld Grimke, these women constructed dramatic representations of black women's lives as they were actually lived. For the women who wrote of urban life, and some of those who wrote about rural life, this often meant writing plays that had little to do with overt racism and the interactions between their communities and white communities, but rather concentrated on the personal relationships of people within the community. Others, such as Georgia Douglas Johnson, dealt with the complex series of relationships between whites and blacks that developed in the South after slavery . When white playwrights investigated these relationships, they included the relationship between the mammy and her "white children," although they focused on the white children. In Johnson's work, the often detrimental effects of those interactions are dramatized.

One of Johnson's earlier plays, *A Sunday Morning in the South* (1926), tells the story of Sue Jones, a woman of seventy who cares for her two grandsons, Tom and Bossie. When we first see Sue, she is wearing the mammy's costume; she wears "a red bandanna handkerchief on her grey head, a big blue gingham apron tied around her waist and big wide old lady comfort shoes" (Perkins 1989: 31). Johnson's choice of words makes an effort to dignify the image, because while Sue wears the uniform of the stereotype, she is not a mammy. She and her neighbor Liza sit and have coffee and discuss the whites in town, who are agitated because there was an attack on a white woman the previous evening, allegedly by a black man. Johnson carefully establishes an alibi for Tom, who is nineteen, early in the scene. Their warm Sunday morning is interrupted by a police officer and the woman who was attacked; the two enter Sue's home looking for Tom. It is apparent that the police have decided Tom is the guilty party. They convince the woman to say that it was Tom, and he agrees to go off with the police.

Sue is at a loss for a way to help her grandson and decides to call in a favor and ask the judge's daughter, whom she nursed, to help get Tom released. She tells her friend Matilda, "Tell Miss Vilet her ole nuse Sue is callin on her and don't fail me" (Perkins 1989: 36). Sue puts her faith in her former employer, hoping that she will be able to save her grandson; unfortunately, they lynch Tom before Matilda can even get to the judge's house.

In this short play, Johnson places Sue in a situation not unlike that of many black women of the rural South. The play emphasizes the danger that white lynch mobs posed for blacks, especially when the virtue of white women was seemingly in jeopardy. Unlike the white-created mammies of the period, Sue's life is not focused on that of the white family for whom she once worked. Sue hopes that the woman for whom she cared will be able to save Tom because the woman's father is a judge. The law offers Sue no protection, a fact of which she is well aware.

The character of Sue refutes another aspect of the stereotypical mammy, that of the domineering woman. Johnson is able, even in this short play, to show the care and concern that Sue has for her grandsons. She encourages Tom to go to school to become a lawyer; there is also an awareness, both on her part and Tom's, that his life is constantly threatened. In 1924, the year in which the play takes place, there is nothing that can prevent the lynching. Later, in the early 1930s, Johnson wrote *Blue-Eyed Black Boy*. Reinvoking the lynching theme, this play centers around the false accusation of an assault on a white woman by a black man. In contrast to other plays, Pauline Waters as the black mother is able to save her son because his father is the white governor; her son even has his father's blue eyes. Pauline's character is much like Sue's, despite the fact that Pauline is younger. She functions as the protector of her children, and reflecting the change in times, is able to stop the lynch mob from killing her son.

By the 1930s, black women were able to more effectively protect their children from white racist violence. The method of that protection shifted dramatically from that of *Rachel,* where the options were limited to enduring the indignity of racism or dying. It had also progressed beyond the situation in *Sunday Morning,* where the only option was a futile appeal to white authority. While Pauline is still required to appeal through the patriarchal white figure (in this case the literal as well as the figurative father of the child), the stakes are higher for the white man. The governor intervenes out of a sense of responsibility and because the young man was falsely accused. His role is substantially different from that of the Confederate soldiers of *The Birth of a Nation,* who save the poor mammy from the evils of black men. The governor acknowledges his paternity (albeit secretly), and it is his responsibility to save the black man from the raging mobs of white men.

Pauline, in her aggressiveness, is strikingly different from the images of black women in the works of Lillian Hellman or Margaret Mitchell, even though all three works were written during the same period. Hellman's Addie lives in a world twenty-four years earlier than Pauline, and Mitchell's Mammy exists in a world that is fifty years earlier. While Hellman does not wish to glorify the Old South, her play recreates images of the caring black servant. Mitchell's book and the film that grew from it were intended to recall the wonderful old days of the South, the gentility of white plantation owners, and the happiness of the slaves before the Civil War. The choice to situate these two stories firmly in past days contrasts sharply with Johnson's decision to set her play in contemporary times.

As the century progressed, blacks would seek more economic and educational opportunities, and political and social change. With the coming of World War II, many more black women were employed, taking jobs that had been abandoned by white women temporarily moving into white men's jobs that paid better. During the late 1930s and early 1940s, more and more unions were formed, particularly in the South and in jobs that were traditionally held by blacks, such as manufacturing and farming. By 1944, the

Southern Regional Council had been formed to improve relations between blacks and whites. Its goals included decreasing lynchings and working slowly toward the "integration [of blacks] into the mainstream of American life" (Giddings 1984: 239). Increased prosperity and education for African Americans led to increased pressure on state and federal governments for more civil rights. Women were, as before, at the forefront of the struggle, as demonstrated by Rosa Parks's famous Birmingham bus ride. Women also helped to organize the Southern Christian Leadership Committee and the Student Nonviolent Coordinating Committee (SNCC); they fought on the front lines of individual and community struggles.

Mother figures became increasingly important during the early days of the civil rights movement. Giddings states that "it was Black women who represented both moral and social authority when controversial decisions had to be made" (1984: 284). The church women of the South provided much needed guidance and support to those who were active. "These women were often looked up to by the whole community because of their wisdom, tenacity, strength, and ability to transcend the oppressive nature of their lives. Wherever the SNCC volunteers stationed themselves in the rural South, such women were invaluable allies" (284). As had been their role for centuries, black women functioned as nurturers of the community as well as of their immediate families. They housed the black student protesters of the SNCC, mothering them in the absence of their own mothers. In the 1950s, Mahalia Jackson commented:

> I believe that right now down South behind most of those brave colored school children and college students you'll find there is still a Negro mother telling them to hold their heads up . . . I hear people talking about the Communists being behind the colored students . . . it's Negro mothers who believe it's time for their children to fight for their rights and a good education. (quoted in Lerner 1972: 585)

By the late 1950s, the strength of black women as nurturers of the race had been recognized in the community, due to the early efforts of club women and educators. It is from this tradition of motherhood that Lorraine Hansberry drew for her first play, *A Raisin in the Sun*. While there has been much criticism of Hansberry's play as integrationist (rather than revolutionary), and while Mama often was and sometimes still is seen as the embodiment of the mammy type who rules the roost, it is evident that Lena Younger is a 1959 reality-based example of the nurturing, protecting, and fighting black woman.

In the original Broadway production and the filmed version, much of the focus of the play was pulled away from the women of the play, and focused instead on Walter Younger and his dreams. When the center of the play is shifted to Walter, his goals and dreams become the most important, and Mama, Beneatha, and Ruth then become the embodiment of the infamous matriarchs of Moynihan's report, domineering and oppressive to the men of the house. Their caution, dreams, and efforts pale against the patriarchal figure who, in an adoption of the white capitalist model, is meant to make the decisions of the house and to rule his women. In Walter's view, the success of the family depends on him, and it is measured by his financial success and becoming his own boss, even and especially if he makes money at the expense of his own people. Because Walter's dream copies that of the white American dream, the play can be interpreted as a "universal" American story. The emphasis is thus pulled away from race, and white audiences feel that they can see a flattering imitation of themselves in the characters.

The women of this play, when examined, clearly do not embody Moynihan's matriarch. Tim Bond's thirty-fifth anniversary production of the play at the Seattle Group Theatre in September 1994 balances the focus of the play, restoring much of its feminist and revolutionary flavor. Lena is proud of her family, but discouraged by the limited opportunities available to them. She encourages Beneatha to go to medical school and become a doctor, because it is an opportunity for her daughter to "climb." She wishes for a better life for Ruth, Walter, and Travis; the small apartment they all share was never meant to be a home to all of them. In leading her children out of the ghetto, her goal is not integration with whites. Lena says, "Son—I just tried to find the nicest place for the least amount of money for my family" (Hansberry 1988: 81). Walter does not feel this way; instead, he regards her use of the money to buy a house as a betrayal. There will not be enough money for him to invest in the liquor store, and another dream is deferred.

As Lena explains, she feels that it is morally wrong to make money by selling alcohol to their depressed community. Her action is calculated to support the black community, whereas Walter's scheme emphasizes the dominant capitalist credo in which a man's making money and financial success are the most important goals. Lena is acutely aware of the difficulties faced by black men in American society, particularly Walter's sense of emasculation because of his limited circumstances. This is also a place for Hansberry to critique capitalism; there cannot be "success" for Walter in the classic American sense, i.e., financial success at the expense of someone else. Lena, from her position as a black woman, lacks the power necessary to completely heal his emotional pain. Ruth is also wary of Walter's potential business partners, and for good reason; the money that he invests is stolen by one of his business associates. Like Lena, Ruth wants to help Walter out of his desolation, but she too is unable to give him what he needs. Walter must find for himself the importance of freedom, family, dignity, and community in order to achieve true manhood.

The money that comes into the family does technically belong to Lena, as it is insurance money from her husband's death. She could have used all of the money on herself, as Ruth suggests early in the play, but she chooses to give part of it to her children to help make their lives easier. In this, she embodies the self-sacrificing mother figure. In the Seattle Group Theatre production, the actress playing Lena physically demonstrated the toll that the years have taken on her. Her physical actions were slow, and had a quality of tiredness. She did not stoop her shoulders, but there was a palpable sense of a great weight on her. Lena's dreams are the ones that have been deferred, after all; without the insurance money, they would have "dr[ied] up like a raisin in the sun" (Hughes, quoted in Hansberry 1988: 3). Lena tells Ruth of her arrival in their small apartment, with the intention of staying for less than a year—a year that turned into decades. Her dreams of living in a house that she and Big Walter owned were never to come to fruition. With the insurance check, Lena finally has the opportunity to achieve some of her own dreams: to live in a comfortable home, to provide Beneatha money for medical school, to help Walter establish himself and assume his manhood in a positive way.

Like the mothers who cared for the SNCC volunteers, Lena is not a stranger to struggle. "Once upon a time," says Lena, "freedom used to be life—now it's money" (Hansberry 1988: 61). The values of her generation were focused elsewhere; while they were to a degree on the community, they were also invested in escaping the conditions of the South. In Lena's value system, which follows the traditional value system of black women and Hansberry's own Marxist values, dignity and family are the most important parts of life; money is important only for its ability to maintain both dignity and family. These values influence Lena's decision to buy the house in Clybourne Park, despite the opposition she knows she will encounter from the whites who live there.

Unlike the matriarchs of Moynihan's imagination, Lena understands the sacrifices that her son has had to make in a world that will not allow him his dreams. Walter is blind to his mother's understanding; he is unable to see beyond his immediate desire for money, thinking that it will gain him the power and respect he desires. He takes his anger out on the women around him; in a conversation with his son, he voices his desire to step into the position of the white patriarch.

In a scene that was not in either the Broadway production or the film version, Ruth and Lena discuss with their neighbor, Mrs.

Johnson, the peril into which they are moving. Mrs. Johnson brings in a paper with news of a family that was bombed out of their house in a white neighborhood. The conversation moves on to Lena's children; when Mrs. Johnson claims that there's "nothing wrong with being a chauffeur," Lena counters with

> There's plenty wrong with it. . . . My husband always said being any kind of a servant wasn't a fit thing for a man to have to be. He always said a man's hands was made to make things, or to turn the earth with—not to drive nobody's car for 'em—or—carry they slop jars. And my boy is just like him—he wasn't meant to wait on nobody. (Hansberry 1988: 139–40)

The Seattle production could not include this scene; the financial situation of the theatre could not allow for the hiring of another actress to play Mrs. Johnson. However, because of the efforts of the director and actress, the sentiment of this speech is embodied by Lena in her interactions with Walter. She is critical of her son's acquiescence to the white capitalist patriarchal system, which she views as disruptive and destructive to her family. Walter has assumed that his mother was just trying to run his life and that she didn't understand what his struggles were as a black man, but she had a better grasp of the situation than he himself did. The omission of this scene in other productions and in the film weakens Lena's character; when she is unable to voice her political and economic consciousness, she becomes more interpretable as a stereotypical mammy. Instead of the strength of the history of black women activists behind her, Lena appears conservative and complicitous with white supremacy.

Lena has spent her life expecting more; she does not intend to take the money offered by the people of Clybourne Park. None of her actions are calculated to please whites, nor is she satisfied with substandard housing or employment. The role has great potential for critiquing the American capitalist system and the detrimental effects it has on African Americans. There is also room for the presentation of the role of Lena Younger as a counterimage of the Moynihan/white imaginary icon of the mammy/matriarch. It is a stark contrast to Annie in *Imitation of Life* (1959); Lena would never tell her children that they must keep to their places.

In George C. Wolfe's *The Colored Museum*, we can see the mythology of the mammy at work. Wolfe's Mama admonishes her son, when he returns from a hard day dealing with "The Man," to "wipe your feet" (Leverett and Richards 1988: 205), drawing directly on Ruth's comments for Walter to "eat your eggs" when he makes a similar complaint. Domineering Mama ignores the struggles of black men. Wolfe also seats Mama, "well-worn," on a couch, reading an oversized Bible. Hansberry's Ruth reappears as a parody of one of the characters in Ntozake Shange's *for colored girls who have considered suicide/when the rainbow is enuf*, the Lady in Plaid (1977). Of course, the Lady in Plaid's final line for this segment of the scene is "Not my babies. He dropped them" (207), a direct reference to Shange's Lady in Red mourning her husband's dropping her children from the fifth storey window. The point of the segment comes with Son's speech:

> Wait one damn minute! This is my play. It's about me and the Man. It ain't got nuthin' to do with no ancient temples on the Nile and it ain't got nuthin' to do with Hestia's bosom. And it ain't got nuthin' to do with you slappin' me across no room. [His gut-wrenching best] It's about me. Me and my pain! My pain! (Leverett and Richards 1988: 208)

As Wolfe's creation shows, Hansberry's play has been interpreted in such a way that it serves to reinforce the mammy icon, rather than disperse it, as was Hansberry's intent.

Margins and Myths

It is clear, through the examples here, that there is a marked difference between the images of African American women in nurturing roles and those in mammy roles. One of the primary reasons for this difference stems from the perspectives from which the fictional women's lives are created. In the representations of whites, black women are constructed as they are seen through the veils of racism and sexism. Their knowledge of the lives of African Americans is restricted by their limited interactions with blacks, and to the historical images with which they are familiar from mass culture. The black woman's experience, if it appears at all, is universalized. The women exist as though they have no life outside of service to whites.

The black women in white narratives are almost always marginalized; except for the example of McCullers's *The Member of the Wedding*, they are never the center. The black woman's place is always that of helper, protector, or defender of the central characters, who in the case of the mammy figure, are white women. From their peripherality, black women are never in a position to speak their own minds. Their manners, speech, and actions are created to be what whites want them to be.

Works by African American women playwrights contrast those of whites; the images on which black women rely to create their visions are those of their experiences or their communities. Within a broad range of experiences, African American women playwrights maintain the commonalities that do exist among them; their characters, regardless of their era, class, or region, must struggle against white male supremacy. This is a constant, from Grimke's play through to Hansberry's.

These plays also reflect the change in mothering and nurturing roles through history. The desperation felt by Rachel in 1916, and the choices she makes in nurturing the race are different from those of Sue or Pauline, ten or twenty years later, or of Lena's forty years later. There is a profound lack of nostalgia; all the playwrights have written plays that reflect contemporary challenges to their lives. Romanticization and sentimentality are absent, whereas it is pervasive in the films and plays of whites of the same periods. They make clear the discrepancy between the mythological concept of the mammy and the reality of black mothers' lives. Unfortunately, this distinction is not always obvious, and it can be obscured when these dramas are directed in ways that do not critique the dominant culture. The staging, film, and subsequent reception of Hansberry's play exemplify this phenomenon; Mama/Lena was transformed from a strong intelligent mother into an irritating ignorant matriarch who embodied the stereotype.

The icon of the mammy is, without doubt, a myth created in the white imagination, and is conveyed by the discourses of theatre and film, and widely disseminated. Mammy appears, as Roland Barthes would say, "both like a notification and like a statement of fact" (1957: 124). Interpretation of the myth as a fact seeps through the entire culture, where it is in turn transformed into fact. That is, mammy becomes a cultural code, determining how real black women are seen. Even those who perceive some of this racist/sexist mythology can be blind to other aspects of it; Amiri Baraka's early critiques of *A Raisin in the Sun* view the play through the eyes of the dominant culture rather than through the culture for whom it was created: African Americans. He reevaluated his earlier opinions in an essay published in the twenty-fifth anniversary edition of *A Raisin in the Sun* (Nemiroff 1987), acknowledging the revolutionary content in Hansberry's play.

The mammy icon conveys the message that the ideal position of black women is to support and care for white women and children. The mammy's role must always be that of supporter; she is not the active individual, and she is never granted her own womanhood and seldom her own family. If the mammy does have a family, the children of the family for which she works are given higher priority than the children of her own body. She is also in a position to take advantage of her superior place close to the white family. There are benefits to be gained, it is rumored, and she must encourage the favor of white men and women. The mammy is also comic. She rarely appears serious, but frequently provides comic relief in the serious situations of whites. She is rarely taken seriously by white characters; Scarlett banters with Mammy, exposing Mam-

my's threats as empty. She cannot be trusted with important decisions, because she is childlike; instead she must look to whites for
guidance.

Yet mammy is also perceived as a threat to society and order.
While much of the time not taken seriously, she can also be seen as
the seed that could bring down the natural order. Primarily
through her role as domineering wife, she threatens the traditional
nuclear family, which has become increasingly important as a way
of regulating society. She is frequently seen raising her children
alone, as in Moynihan's report, driving off men who might otherwise have been able to function as her protector. This woman wants
no protector, thus ultimately must fail in her attempts to protect
her own children. In both of the mainstream films from the 1950s,
Imitation of Life and *The Member of the Wedding*, the controlling
black mother is unable to properly care for her children, and she
leaves them to their own ruin. In the 1990s, as the media image of
the inner-city single parent, she is blamed for continuing poverty,
gang violence, and rising pregnancy rates among teens.

As a matriarch, she becomes a threat to male power, particularly that of black males. In many mainstream images discussed
here, mammies are seen taking control of men, and the alleged
threat to the nuclear family is psychologically interpreted as a castrating presence. Mammy now appears to desire power for its own
sake, especially power over black men. From the mammy of *The
Birth of a Nation*, who puts that Northern servant in his place, to
the portrayals of Addie in *The Little Foxes* and Mammy in *Gone
With the Wind*, the image persists of the black woman being in
control of black men. For white men, she is a threat because of her
courage and strength; history has many examples of black women
who defied white male supremacy by agitating against slavery, taking action in political processes, and working to create an alternative to the white male supremacist capitalist culture. She is also
threatening because of white male desire for her exoticism; she is
the instrument through which white men create children who may

eventually be able to pass as white, usurping white power and privilege.

As the century wore on, this icon also began to cause deep splits within the black community. The image of the mammy who was more concerned with whites than her own children, who emasculated her man, and who wished to retain the status quo was presented as reality and accepted as such by many black men. Whereas in previous decades black women had been at the forefront of social and political change, during the 1960s they were pushed into the background. The public focus of the civil rights struggle was on black men; women were often kept from taking positions of authority within the movement. When black women asked about their rights, they were told they would have to wait until the black man was free. Unfortunately, the mammy icon's wide distribution as truth by the Moynihan report included the black community. The icon served as an effective tool of a divide-and-conquer strategy to stifle the aggressive tactics of the civil rights movement. The historical tradition of mothers, nurturers, educators, and protectors in the black community was belittled or forgotten, and instead became associated with the images of the mammy.

Two more recent works by African American women also point to the effort still being made to rehabilitate the image of the black mother/nurturer. In Suzan-Lori Parks's play, *The Death of the Last Black Man in the Whole Entire World* (see Mahone 1994), one of the main characters is Black Woman with Fried Drumstick. Audience members noting the character names in the program will likely expect the character Black Woman with Fried Drumstick to be the embodiment of the mammy. Yet instead of a mammy, they have a woman in the process of remembering her history and performing the final nurturing task, that of preparing her husband's body for burial. Throughout Parks's play, there are historical images that are *animated* so that they may tell their stories, write their histories, and be included; they also disempower the images imposed by whites. This rewriting of history, this representation of images, will save black people from the fate of invisibility, for, "if you dont write it down then they will come along and tell the future that we did not exist" (Mahone 1994: 252).

Julie Dash has also presented alternative images in her film *Daughters of the Dust* (1991). As in the tradition of black women writing about black women's lives, there are mothers but no mammies. There is a "matriarch." However, Dash not only used the term to mean the female head of a family (a role that Nana Peazant takes on as her duty as the "last of the old"), but also consciously avoided casting a physical mammy type in the role of Nana Peazant. Dash is able to focus on the nurturing that Nana performs, and thus to return a long-standing tradition to the place of honor it should occupy. She is a protector and a guardian of her extended family, showing them how to keep memories of the past and traditions of the culture that will sustain them in the future.

African American women continue to recall and retell history and to remember the stories and lives of the mothers and nurturers who supported and fought for communities. Despite this, mammies have continued to surface in popular culture; Nell Carter's role in the mid–1980s sitcom *Gimme A Break* revives the black mammy who cares for the young white girls in their passage to womanhood. Fortunately, the presence of the iconic mammy has decreased in the past few years; instead, filmmakers and playwrights have consciously avoided using the icon in favor of more complex, subtle representations. A few of them, like the film starring Whoopi Goldberg entitled *Corrina, Corrina* (1994), subvert the expectations of the audience by using a standard mammy situation and reshaping it. Goldberg's character very clearly has a life away from the white Jewish family for which she works, a life to which she exposes the young girl in her care. Goldberg ends the film quitting her job, involved in a love relationship with the Jewish man for whom she had worked. However, some of the behavioral signs of mammyhood are visible. While there is a realistic setup for the situation, we ultimately have Whoopi, as Corrina, taking over the nurturing of her young motherless charge, occasionally going against the wishes of the child's father. Corrina does have a family, but she is in conflict with that family because of her concern for the girl, as well as for her later involvement with her employer. Whoopi doesn't don the mammy's costume, but she certainly functions as a mammy.

Other films maintain the mammy's role without using the visual cues as well. These mammies are not large women, nor do they wear the standard costume. bell hooks asserts that Neil Jordan's *Mona Lisa* has a character that is, despite all outward appearances, a mammy. Mona Lisa is a lesbian; "Yet her choice of a female partner does not mean sexual fulfillment as the object of her lust is a drug-addicted young white woman who is always too messed up to be sexual. Mona Lisa nurses and protects her. Rather than asserting sexual agency, she is once again in the role of mammy" (hooks 1992: 74). While it may be argued that hooks does not engage many of the film's larger issues with this statement, the character of Mona Lisa inarguably embodies key elements of the mammy figure. The social role that the icon mammy plays in mainstream culture has not changed, but the presentation of the woman who performs as mammy has.

Chapter 2

Mulattas, Tragedy, and Myth

She most often begins as a sweet girl. So close to white that she fools whites, she is given a place of honor by her darker brothers and sisters. She is naturally refined, through blood rather than environment. Sweet and charming as she is, there courses through her veins a single drop of black blood that, given time, will bring her whole world crashing down around her. Thwarted from gaining her aspirations, a desperate fate awaits her. Suicide is the only way out.

This is one of the narratives of the tragic mulatta, that mythic woman who is always (and only) a mixture of black and white. In the above scenario, she is virginal and innocent and would remain so if she did not aspire higher than she should. The blackness within, no matter how small a fraction, means that she cannot have complete access to the white world. There is also the bad tragic mulatta; she, like the good girl, passes for white. She grows to despise her race and her family and seeks to use her skin color to escape the life that would otherwise be her destiny. She is mean, angry, and occasionally violent, as well as bitter, sullen, shadowy, and untrustworthy. Her heathen black blood eventually boils up in her and spoils everything. Like the sweet mulatta, her fate must also be tragic; she too must die, whether by her own hand or someone else's. If such a fate should be averted, her life will nevertheless be one of pain and sorrow.

Like the myth of the mammy, the two-sided myth of the tragic mulatta has its origins in the minstrel show. The mulatta did appear in the white-in-blackface minstrel shows of the early nine-teenth century. The mulatta is more refined than the dark-skinned mammy because of her white blood; she lacks the exaggerated lips and nose and is dressed better, wearing a hat instead of the trade-mark kerchief of the darker-skinned woman. She is judged more conventionally beautiful because of her smaller features and size. There is still something wild about her, though, and more than a hint of coquettishness.

The mulatta, being a woman, can be tragic, whereas the mu-latto cannot. This "black blood" that is the primary defining char-acteristic of the mulatta and mulatto appears in their behavior. The woman once believed white (chaste) becomes sexually available in the way that black women are. For white men, the mulatta is the body of a white woman imbued with the mythic sexuality of black women. The mulatto, accordingly, takes on the mythic aggressive sexuality—in the active rather than the passive sense—of the black man. Thus, he cannot be tragic; his sexual advances toward white women equal rape and miscegenation. A child must be defined by the race of its mother, so that the child of a white woman by a black father must be "white"; but that "white" is not pure. This infraction by the black man/mulatto must be punished by death because it has "polluted" whiteness.

One of the elements of the tragedy surrounding the mulatta is her lack of access to power and her essentially female position. Her racialized state puts her in a position that, in a racist culture, equals powerlessness, despite her "blood," which, in the terms of such a discourse, is by vast majority "white." Her powerlessness becomes complete within the American patriarchal matrix as well. Unlike the mulatto, then, she is denied access by virtue of both her race (or trace thereof) and her gender. Where the mulatto allegedly has some power because of his gender (and his ability to exercise sexual power over white women), the mulatta remains, because of her "taint," bereft of agency (see Gordon 1996b).

We can see evidence of the worst of the stereotypes in D. W. Griffith's *The Birth of a Nation* (1915). Here we have both mulatto and mulatta, both from the North, by association embodying the worst aspects of their dual heritage. If whites in the North are perceived as supporting the abolition of slavery, it follows in the racist logic of the film that they would be less strict with their servants. It might also follow that white women in the North would choose to become sexually involved with black men, resulting in mulattoes who would carry on the mother's arrogance. In the North, then, it appears that blacks are permitted to take privileges reserved for whites in the South.

Silas Lynch is an example of the mean-spirited mulatto who is allowed to exercise some power and as a result aspires to what is above him. His desire for the genteel white woman is a threat to white men. As a mulatto, he is even worse than the black men who come to the South with the Union army, because his "white blood" gives him audacity. Silas cannot be tragic because he is male.

Griffith's mulatta is the bad mulatta. She is a servant, but a servant in a Northern household is not the obedient black of the South. Because most of the story takes place in the South, there are few scenes that include this mulatta. She herself may not be tragic, but Griffith explains that in her feisty and deceitful way, she causes much of the tragedy of the nation. Stonewall's servant is disobedient and disrespectful, showing none of the subservience that one of her rank should show. She does as she pleases, and plots against the Southerners who have come to meet with Stonewall. She has an encounter with a Southern congressman who has come to this meeting. When he requests that she perform some servant's function, she haughtily refuses him. She argues with him and he leaves, disgusted by her effrontery.

After the Southern congressman leaves, she tears at her clothing in what seems a very sexual way and throws herself on the floor, and this tantrum draws the attention of Stonewall. Griffith refers to the exchange between Stonewall and this female servant as "a leader's weakness that blots a nation." The servant manages to convince Stonewall that the Southerner has attempted to take sexual advantage of her, hence the tearing of her clothes. He consoles her, angry at the liberty this man has attempted to take with this woman. The evil mulatta is able to convince Stonewall that the Southern system is evil, as this obscenity is something that Southern white men do regularly. In the film, the incident influences Stonewall to give a position of authority to the mulatto Silas Lynch, who later goes South and becomes part of the carpetbaggers' evil regime.

The threat from those of mixed race is made explicit in Griffith's film; considering the theme of the film, this is not unexpected. Explicitly white supremacist in nature, the film encourages the belief that blacks are the source of America's problems, and that mulattoes are not exempt from blame. In fact, the mulattoes of this film are much more to blame for problems than even the evil marauding black men, because their white blood makes them aspire to things they should not. They are dangerous because they will continue to identify themselves as blacks against whites, and because their access to white privilege (both mulattoes have Stonewall's ear) gives them access to power over whites (Silas in the carpetbaggers' regime, the mulatta in her false accusation against the Southern congressman). These mulattoes are not portrayed as tragic because of their acceptance of their race, but because of their complicity in trying to destroy white culture.

Of all the images of African American women, the image of the mulatta, tragic or not, is the most complex one. Unlike the mammy, the mulatta figure changes drastically through time and communities. The consistency of the representations of the mammy and mother is absent from the material on mulattas. In one sense, the mulatta lies outside the dualism of Western imagination; she is neither white nor black, yet she is both black and white (see Zack 1993). In the reality of the American (or even Western) racial context, however, she can only be black, even if she passes for white. The antiblack racial context does not allow for any other position. In early white representations, she is a physicalization of racial mixing, a dilution of the purity of white blood. For African Americans during the early twentieth century, she was a constant visual reminder of the sexual slavery of black women, who for so long had been at the sexual disposal of their masters. To the white wife of the slave master, she was a reminder of the sexual liaisons her spouse had with his slaves.

The mulatta was also seen as the potential savior of her people; her limited access to education, money, and influence should be used to better her black community of origin, or so it was thought by whites. When occupying such a position, she is either treated as superior by other blacks or disdained or resented by those with darker skin because her life as the master's favored is easier than theirs. Added to this complexity, there is also the issue of "passing." Blacks are ambivalent about light-skinned people passing as white. On the one hand, passing is seen as having an unfair advantage; by virtue of skin color, one who is born "black" gains access to white privilege. The person who passes must dissociate herself or himself from the black community, so that her or his family origins remain a secret. This amounts to abandonment of family and friends, adding to the level of resentment.

On the other hand, those who pass can fool whites and are thereby able to occupy a place of power. Those whites invested in white supremacy feel that only those whose blood is pure are worthy of white power and privilege. Blacks sometimes see passing as a powerful move, even as it requires a loss of friends and family. Passing has also created a situation where some blacks look at whiteness as suspect; in their experience, family members who have passed create families of "whites" who are really "black." As we shall see, the perceptual categories of race of "black" and "white" break down not only in situations like this, but in representation as well.

The analysis of the mammy icon reveals a marked difference between the portrayals written by whites versus those authored by blacks. The mulatta is both treated and envisioned differently in plays by African American women than in mainstream representation, but in many cases the element of tragedy still exists in the mulatta characters of black women playwrights. The primary difference between the white and black representations of the mulatta is in the nature of the tragedy. In the white imagination, which equates black with evil, any element of tragedy that comes to the mulatta is a result of the blackness within her. Her "mark of Cain" becomes her tragic flaw. By contrast, for many African American women playwrights, the tragedy originates in the circumstance of her origin; often the mulatta is the result of her black mother's rape. In other more contemporary works, her tragedy stems from her inability to reconcile the two sides of her racial heritage, or to find a space outside the dualism in which she can comfortably exist.

Mulattas

Zoe, the mulatta character in Dion Boucicault's 1859 play *The Octoroon*, is a sweet tragic mulatta. Boucicault's play was lauded in its day for its progressive representation of blacks. The author does give a human and highly dignified presentation of Zoe, and his presentation of the other slaves is not as repulsive as in the work of his contemporaries. Zoe is the nearly white illegitimate daughter of a plantation owner. Because of her proximity to her father, she has been treated more as a family member than as their property. In fact, Zoe's father has left provisions in his will that she will be freed upon his death.

Zoe's white features make her attractive to the white men around her. Her cousin George has recently returned from Paris and is not aware of Zoe's taint; he falls in love with her. She does not immediately tell him of her origins, an action that eventually leads to her tragic fate. For the Peyton family, Zoe's incipient relationship with George is the least of the problems. Because of debts and taxes, the plantation is to be auctioned off, and because of a legal mix-up, Zoe is considered a part of the property. Zoe's status is ambiguous; the other slaves treat her as though she were white. She is addressed by the slave Dido as "Missey Zoe" (Boucicault 1859: 6), yet Dora, a white neighbor, treats her as a servant.

George is confused, because no one has told him about Zoe's situation.

When George professes his love to Zoe, she is shocked. She realizes that he is unaware of her mother's race; he knows only that she is illegitimate. In Act 2, she responds to his proposal, "George, you cannot marry me; the laws forbid it" (16). Her description of the telltale evidence of her true race shows the extent to which she is ashamed of this:

> That is the ineffaceable curse of Cain. Of the blood that feeds my heart, one drop in eight is black—bright red as the rest may be, that one drop poisons all the flood; those seven bright drops give me love like yours—hope like yours—ambition like yours—life hung with passions like dew-drops on the morning flowers; but the one black drop gives me despair, for I'm an unclean thing—forbidden by the laws—I'm an Octoroon! (16–17)

The dualistic myth of the differences between black and white is blatant: the "seven bright drops" contrast the "one black drop." It taints her fingernails and eyes with a "bluish tinge" (16) that is visible to all. Love, hope, and ambition are reserved for whites, and except for that one poison drop, Zoe should have had all the things George has. Zoe demonstrates the extent to which it is accepted throughout her culture that blackness is a taint, unclean, and even poison, because she uses these words to describe herself. Her bit of blackness also makes her more sexually accessible in the eyes of some white men, namely the evil M'Closky. "That one black drop of blood burns in her veins and lights up her heart like a foggy sun," he declares, after overhearing Zoe and George's conversation (17).

Zoe, George, and Mrs. Peyton are all surprised at the sale of the plantation to hear that because there was a lien against the property at the time Peyton ordered Zoe's freedom, she is not really free. She is distraught at the thought of being sold, but is indeed sold at auction to M'Closky. The papers that would relieve her of this fate have been lost in the mail, with the aid of M'Closky. The mail is eventually recovered, and M'Closky is caught in his deceit by a camera. Unfortunately, Zoe has already planned to take her own life, and gets poison from one of the slaves. She dies just as it is revealed that George is indeed the master of the plantation, and that she was free after all.

Zoe is differentiated from the other blacks on the plantation through several means. As Boucicault describes in the stage directions, Zoe wears a white muslin dress, while the slave women wear striped skirts, calico jackets, and the occasional kerchief. While the play's action is not reminiscent of the minstrel show that was its contemporary, the division remains between two basic types of black female characters—the large mammy and the beautiful mulatta. There is also a marked difference between the speech of the slave women and that of Zoe. She speaks in the refined language of the whites, while the women marked as black by their costume are also marked by their use (or misuse) of language. Because of her proximity to whiteness, and in the relatively honored position of an octoroon, she has had the education of a white woman, despite the limitations society has set upon her. She is, as a result, deserving of white sympathy, because she is closer to whiteness. The use of the mulatta as an appeal to whites was not unknown during this period, and one of the elements ensuring the success of Harriet Beecher Stowe's *Uncle Tom's Cabin* (1852) was her use of the mulatta to elicit sympathy.

Thus Zoe, by her dress and language, is distinguished from the other black women on the plantation, and judging from her dialogue, she feels more white than black. Her blackness is a taint on what would otherwise be delicate Southern white womanhood. While not explicit in the text, it is implicit that Zoe, because of her heritage, is of a higher class than the field hands. There is no animosity from the other blacks on the plantation against Zoe; those who are hostile toward her are the whites, whose territory she seems ready to invade. In other words, her threat is not against other blacks, but against whites. If she passes for white, then she could continue to disseminate her despised black blood throughout the pure white race through her marriage to George.

Zoe's death is tragic partially because she is a good, sweet, honest character. She does not hide her race, and several times during the course of the play she refers to herself as being a part of a "we" that is black. In fact, had Zoe refused to marry George, she might not have had to commit suicide. The good mulatta will admit the truth of her heritage, which Zoe certainly does. She does not infringe upon white privilege, but remains in her "place." She obeys the orders of her neighbor, and does not seek to be recognized as an equal to whites.

The icon of the tragic mulatta was well established by the middle of the nineteenth century, while the mammy's was not fixed until the late nineteenth and early twentieth centuries. The mulatta's early establishment set a firm base for her evolution in the twentieth century. There are three types of tragic mulatta characters in white-authored fiction of the period 1920–55. One is the divided-soul character who desires a white lover/husband, and suffers a tragic fate as a result. Another is the unhappy passing mulatta who denies her race and dies. The third is the exotic, restless, and mysterious mulatta, who is inherently a sexual character.

The 1949 film *Pinky* is based on the novel *Quality* by Mrs. Cid Rickett Sumner, and involves the first kind of tragic mulatta. However, the film's mulatta comes to a happy end rather than suffering a tragic fate because she embraces her blackness and leaves behind her aspirations of whiteness and assimilation. In the last scene of the film, Pinky stands next to the sign that proclaims her clinic and nursing school, with a glowing smile on her face. She deserves it, because that happiness has been a long time coming.

At the beginning of the film, we find Pinky returning to her family's Southern home, after spending years in New York earning a degree in nursing and becoming engaged to a white doctor. The problems she encounters are created out of her own desires. Her desire for the privilege and power that whiteness will give her leads her to deny her "true race": she is passing for white. She has forgotten what life is like for blacks in the South, having been able, in the North, to avoid questions about her family that would have given away her secret. In fact, Pinky is planning to marry her fiancé and spend the rest of her life as white after her marriage; she has gone by the name Patricia while living her alternate life in New York. Thankfully, through the graciousness of the old white woman for whom her grandmother works and on whose property she lives, Pinky is convinced to take her proper role in society within the black community and to abandon her hopes of becoming white.

Pinky is basically a sweet mulatta; she is kind and compassionate, and only occasionally does she forget her "place" and anger the Southern whites. There is much about her that recalls Boucicault's Zoe, in fact. They both understand the social restrictions upon them, but are willing to go against both law and culture to marry the men they love. While Zoe was able to acknowledge her race, Pinky must hide hers. She does not plan to stay in the South, but once Miss Em becomes ill, Pinky is convinced by her grandmother to nurse the old woman until she dies. Pinky is reluctant, but she takes the unpaid position as a favor to her grandmother.

Pinky also shuns the possibility of a professional association with a young black doctor. He sees her return South as a possibility; he hopes that she will consider starting a nursing school for black women. She is insistent that she is only in town for a short time, and is planning to marry her doctor and return north. His disappointment is evident as she rejects his proposition. The old woman hopes that Pinky will augment her formal education with social education, and will be who she is rather than pretending that she is something she is not. On her deathbed, Miss Em rewrites her will, leaving her house and land to Pinky. Of course, Miss Em's relatives are outraged, and the potential is set for Pinky's development into a tragic mulatta. Pinky has to go to court to prove that she did not influence Miss Em, and a case of national attention is created. Her fiancé, who has by this point been apprised of Pinky's true heritage, finds that his efforts to keep Pinky's race a secret have been nullified by the press. He still wants to marry her, but they would have to move to Colorado in order to avert public embarrassment to his family.

Pinky takes the case to court and eventually wins the right to keep her property. Implicit in this decision is Pinky's acknowledgment that she cannot live her false life. In keeping with Miss Em's expectations of her, she remains in town and converts the house into a nursing school and clinic, helped by the doctor she shunned when she first arrived. Pinky's happiness is assured when she makes the decision to stay in her place and do what she should do. Her action benefits the black community (it now has its own nursing school), and the white (which maintains its "purity"). Happiness and the aversion of tragedy come from her decision to "keep her place" and remove herself from the white world.

Edna Ferber created another tragic mulatta, Julie, who was brought to life on the stage by Oscar Hammerstein II and Jerome Kern in 1927. Like many plays that include a tragic mulatta, *Show Boat* is not her story; Julie is only a character, if a sympathetic one, in the life of Magnolia, the main character of the play. Like Pinky, Julie is passing for white, working as an actress on the showboat *Cotton Blossom*. She is usually a wonderful performer, and is very popular with the audiences. She is loved by all of the crew on the showboat, both black and white. She has a relationship with Queenie, the cook, that could potentially be seen as a mother-daughter relationship much like the one that would be created in *Imitation of Life*. However, only two people know her secret—her white husband, Steve, and Pete, one of the white boat workers. Knowledge of her secret not only would cause her to lose her position as a leading actress, but also would expose her marriage to her white husband as against Mississippi miscegenation laws. Julie shares with Pinky a romantic attachment to a white man, but in Julie's case they have married.

Of course, Julie is a tragic mulatta, so her secret cannot remain so for long. She is discovered and cannot deny her race. Early in the play, she incurs the wrath of Pete, whose desire for her is much like that of M'Closky in *The Octoroon*; his knowledge about her true racial heritage only increases his desire. Pete spies Queenie wearing a brooch he had given to Julie. He questions Queenie, who refuses to tell him who gave it to her, but he knows that Julie did. He confronts Julie about it, and she explains that if Steve were to know of the gift, he would likely fight with Pete because of it. Unfortunately, Steve sees Pete bothering Julie, and they do fight. Because of the fight, Pete is thrown off the boat and vows his revenge on Julie. He steals her picture off a billboard for the night's performance and hurries off to town to get the sheriff. He sees Frank, one of the other actors on the boat, and lets him know of his plans. Fortunately, Ellie, one of the other actresses from the boat, also hears of the plan. Pete reveals to the sheriff that there is a case of miscegenation on board the *Cotton Blossom.*

Ellie hurries back to the boat and alerts Steve that the sheriff is on his way. During rehearsal, Steve tells Julie the news from Ellie, and reveals that he has a plan to save them. Julie faints, and pleads with Captain Andy that she is ill and cannot perform that night. He agrees. Steve engages in a ritual that ensures they will be able to remain together. Just before Pete and the sheriff enter, Steve cuts Julie's finger and sucks the blood from the wound in the presence of much of the crew. Technically, he now has "negro blood" in him, just like Julie, and their marriage is no longer illegal. When the sheriff arrives, Steve explains that he has Negro blood in him. They are not arrested, but Andy is warned not to perform with "mixed-bloods" on his stage. Julie and Steve bid a tearful farewell to the cast and crew of the *Cotton Blossom.*

This segment occupies more than half of the first act of the play. Ostensibly, this sets up both the relationship and the careers of Magnolia and Ravenal. Magnolia has learned all of the lines for the play; Ravenal is in need of both employment and a way out of town. Julie and Steve's dismissal leaves Andy in the lurch for a replacement (the town next on their schedule is a big moneymaker, and the show must go on). Magnolia can, at least temporarily, replace Julie, and Ravenal's love for her transforms them into a popular stage couple. Hammerstein sets Julie as an *imitation*; she is not quite a rival, because of her love for Magnolia. Magnolia's "replacement" of Julie happens only because Julie is not in her "proper" place.

Julie is seen only once again in the play. After Magnolia and Ravenal become successful, they marry and have a child. Ravenal decides to take his family to Chicago, where his "profession" (gambling) has them moving from poverty to splendor and back. Eventually Ravenal uses up what little luck he had. He leaves town, sending Magnolia the last of his money at their one-room tenement in Chicago. Frank and Ellie have come to Chicago to perform at the Trocadero, and happen to meet Magnolia. Seeing Magnolia's poverty, they offer her the chance to audition for the manager. The Trocadero is where Julie works as a singer; in the depths of her melodrama Steve has left her, and she consoles herself by drinking. She is not always reliable, and when we see her, she is close to losing her job. While the manager has some sympathy for her, he has a business to run. As on the *Cotton Blossom*, Julie is extremely popular with the audiences of the Trocadero. She performs one more song—rehearsal for another performance she will never give—before she goes off to her dressing room. Magnolia comes in shortly thereafter with Frank. They convince the manager to give her an audition, and she sings "Can't Help Lovin' Dat Man," which she learned from Julie. The manager is reluctant to hire her (he already has a singer, Julie). Julie, however, has seen Magnolia. She does not announce herself, but listens out of sight. She sacrifices her job for Magnolia, this time of her own accord. She leaves a message for the manager letting him know she is going on a binge (the avoidance of which was the key to her employment), and he has no choice but to hire Magnolia on the spot.

Julie must live out the full term of her tragic fate, because she chose to live in the world as white and married a white man despite the laws and social taboos against it. Even near the end of the play, she still attempts to maintain a place on the fringes of white privilege. She is not even released by an early death, but must grow old in misery for her transgression. Julie and Zoe share another circumstance. In both cases, lower-class white men desire them (Pete and M'Closky) and feel that they have a right to them. The men feel themselves racially superior to the mulattas; both men try to take the women away from their gentlemen (generally middle and upper class) and reveal their true identities (although George is already aware of Zoe's race, M'Closky reveals Zoe's status as slave), thinking it will "lower" the women and thereby give the men access to the mulattas. The forced revelations bring about the demise of both women.

In 1994, *Show Boat* was revived in Canada, and subsequently moved to Broadway, where it won several awards. The production was not without controversy; however, the nature of that controversy exposes interesting attitudes in contemporary America about race and mixed race. The Toronto production met with protest from blacks, who objected to the racist characterizations of the characters Queenie and Joe. There was renewed controversy about Hammerstein's lyrics to "Ol' Man River." When the role was originally performed by Paul Robeson, he changed the lyrics from "Niggers work on the Mississippi" to "Colored folks work on the Mississippi," to Hammerstein's annoyance. In the current revival, there have been vast reductions of the use of the word "nigger" to where, in the eyes of those involved in this production, they are culturally and historically correct. The number that opened Act 2 of the original production, titled "In Dahomey" and performed by a chorus of blacks who pretend to be from Africa for the performance, has been eliminated. No one, however, opposed the character Julie. Lee Israel, writing in *Theater Week*, notes, "We know, from experience (*Carmen Jones*) that Hammerstein has no real concept of blacks; his statements that '[*Show Boat*] has always been good for the Negro' and that blacks 'emerge with honor and respect and affection' are tainted" (28). Lonette McKee, who created this incarnation of the role of Julie and returned for a brief time in 1996, said of her character:

Julie is the classic tragic mulatto. She's forced to do things that would not be socially acceptable to me, right now—or to any other mulatto or mixed person. In those days, your choices were either to be a slave or a servant. Black people, or mixed people were not treated as human beings. Julie was forced to make the decision that she made. (Quoted in Buckley 1994: 17)

That critics did not object to the tragic mulatta as a racist stereotype, as they did with the mammy figure, suggests that the characterization of the woman of mixed race, particularly one who passes for white, is not considered a racist stereotype, or perhaps, that anyone who passes for white deserves what she gets. The production also reveals some change in attitude, for Julie is played by a black woman (McKee here, specifically) in this incarnation. The implications of this will be taken up below.

Black women attempting to pass for white continued to be an issue in mainstream cinema during the 1940s and 1950s. As mentioned in chapter 1, another infamous tale of the mulatta who inserts herself into white culture and usurps white privilege is the 1959 version of *Imitation of Life* (as it was in the 1934 version of the film). Sarah Jane is a bad mulatta, for she vehemently denies any connection to blacks, and forces her way into the white world. She is angry and self-hating, shouting several times that she is not black; her sobbing "I'm white! I'm white!" has the effect of biasing the audience against her and making her an object of pity.

Like Julie, Sarah Jane's refusal to live her life as black can mean only a life of misery for Sarah Jane. She is beaten and nearly raped after her high school boyfriend finds out that she is black. She refuses the help and advice of her mother and runs away from home. Her transgression can only be taken so far; she finds work dancing in clubs, doing work that is just short of prostitution. She does not always enjoy white privilege; her Negro blood makes her a sexual object. Unlike the other women who become sexual objects in the eyes of white men (Zoe, Julie), Sarah Jane takes this position willingly. It is even more apparent with Sarah Jane that her blackness is responsible for her heightened sexuality (which she expresses through dancing). She is restricted in the narrative to positions that inherently lack power.

The discoveries of these three mulattas, Pinky, Julie, and Sarah Jane, are pivotal points within the narratives. Until the time (or, in the case of Pinky, several times) that they are discovered, they are read by the audience as white, and occasionally believe this themselves. All three characters were played by white women with dark hair, although there were probably black women with skin sufficiently light to have played any of the roles; Fredi Washington played Peola in the 1934 version of *Imitation of Life*, for example. Their bodies are reduced to signs of identity, and their difficulties are increased when they are read not as they wish to be read (white) but as they are socially read (black). A complex transferal occurs, for the audience is placed in a position of viewing white as black, emphasizing the danger of the mulatta: she can "infiltrate" white society without being *seen*. The actors playing the mulattas pass for black in the audience's imagination. They exist as a visual representation of that complex space between races and demonstrate the ease with which the Other can find her way into the company, society, and privilege of the Self. The mulatta figures also blur the lines of cultural history and experience. The white women who play these roles carry for the audience none of the history or cultural specificity of blacks, implying that racial specificity can be bred out. Julie is the only character who nearly exposes her secret by doing something culturally "black"; she sings "Can't Help Lovin' Dat Man," whose language and music are marked as black. The visual elision of blackness is contradicted by the narrative, which claims that the mulatta can only be happy (and avoid the tragic fate allotted her) if she grounds herself in her community of origin—the black community.

In the 1994 revival of *Show Boat*, McKee's cultural specificity seems to come through the character, inherently changing the audience's view of Julie and, I would argue, the meaning of the play. McKee's race may not be visually apparent (she could indeed pass for white, at least on stage), but it can be assumed via association. Her biography in the program is filled with references to previous work that is culturally specific (she starred in *Lady Day at Emerson's Bar and Grill*, a play about Billie Holiday, and also worked in several black films). Her "black" roles, mentioned in her biography in the program, inform the audience that *this* "mulatta" is authentic. Because McKee herself is grounded in her community, the subtext to her performance is a happy, "good" mulatta, one who not only "knows her place," but is comfortable there. For blacks in the audience, McKee's cultural specificity is another way into the play, aside from the obviously black characters.

Miscegenation Blues, or the Other Side of the Tragic Mulatta

There are several examples of the mulattas dramatized by black women before 1950. They considered the theme of miscegenation and characterized the mulatta/mulatto as tragic because of the circumstances of her or his birth. Plays by Georgia Douglas Johnson and Zora Neale Hurston provide two perspectives on the dangers of miscegenation for blacks. Both playwrights treated the lives of Southern rural blacks, although with different slants. In both cases, the mulatta characters do not separate themselves from the black community, nor are they thought of as outside of it. This is one of the primary differences between mulatta characterizations of white and black writers.

Johnson wrote two plays involving miscegenation; *Blue Blood* (1926) is the first of these. The situation is ostensibly a happy one; two Southern black women—Mrs. Bush, the working-class mother, and Mrs. Temple, the middle-class mother—are preparing for the marriage of their children. Mrs. Bush's daughter, May, is marrying John Temple, although May is also in love with Randolph Strong. Mrs. Bush would prefer that May marry Randolph, but May has chosen John. Mrs. Bush thinks John is "stuck up," and she "never did believe in two 'lights' marrying, nohow, it's onlucky" (Perkins

1989: 39). Mrs. Temple and Mrs. Bush have the opportunity to spend some time together before the ceremony in a comic scene that plays on class differences between blacks. Mrs. Temple thinks that May isn't good enough for John, and Mrs. Bush thinks John isn't good enough for May. When Mrs. Temple comments on the other girls envying May, Mrs. Bush retorts, "They'd better envy JOHN!!! You don't know who May is; she's got blue blood in her veins" (41). This prompts the mothers' stories of the children's origins. Mrs. Bush brags that Captain McCallister is May's father, hence her "blue blood" and fair skin. This shocks Mrs. Temple, but not simply because she is amazed; she has her own terrible tale to reveal. The tragedy of the tragic mulatta is removed from the children; instead, the tragic characters are their mothers.

While Mrs. Bush believes that "blue blood" (or "white blood") makes her daughter special, she is mistaken; as fate would have it, John and May are brother and sister, for Mrs. Temple was raped by the same Captain McCallister while preparing for her own wedding. "There wasn't any one there that cared enough to help me, and you know yourself, Mrs. Bush, what little chance there is for women like us, in the South, to get justice or redress when these things happen" (43). Her fiancé married her and raised the son that was the result of the rape. Of course, Mrs. Bush and Mrs. Temple can't allow the children to marry, and the revelation of their common progenitor would create a scandal. Fortunately, Randolph Strong returns and he and May decide to escape and marry, saving the face of all concerned. Here, there is no exile or death, providing yet another fundamental difference between white-authored mulatta texts and black-authored texts.

The trauma of Mrs. Temple's rape and the crisis that it caused are mitigated by the amusing class conflict that makes up the majority of this short one-act play. The tragedy of these mulattas is removed from its traditional place—the child of an interracial union, usually the female child—and replaced. As is appropriate for tragicomedy rather than tragedy, the immediate problem of the marriage is resolved. Because of Randolph Strong's intervention (in the form of a dark-skinned man), the scandal of siblings marrying is averted. John, of course, is left without a bride, but he is not a central character and is never seen. In fact, because Mrs. Bush and Mrs. Temple are the center of the play, the tragedy of their situation is centered. The canceled marriage is only a result of the tragic situation of black women who, as Mrs. Temple says, have no recourse against the unwanted attentions of white men. The tragedy—the rape of black women by white men—brings together two women from different classes who otherwise seem to have little in common.

Johnson's other miscegenation play, *Blue-Eyed Black Boy*, has a more immediately positive outcome, although it does not go so far as to support miscegenation. This play was written in the 1930s and was submitted to the Federal Theatre Project for production in the Negro Units, although the script did not see production there. Pauline Waters is a middle-aged woman who is helping her daughter Rebecca prepare for her wedding. Early in the one-act play, we learn that Jack alone of his siblings has blue eyes, and that he is an aspiring intellectual: "Just give him a book and he's happy—says he's going to quit running that crane—and learn engineering as soons you get married" (Perkins 1989: 48). Pauline is waiting for Dr. Grey, her daughter's fiancé. While they are sitting, they hear a commotion outside. A neighbor enters and informs them that Jack has been arrested for allegedly "brush[ing] up against a white woman" (49). The white members of the community are set on lynching him. Pauline quickly comes up with a plan to save her son from the lynch mob; she will appeal to the governor to save him. She tells Dr. Grey:

> Here Tom take this [small ring], run jump in your horse and buggy and fly over to Governor Tinkhem's house and don't let nobody—nobody stop you. Just give him the ring and say, Pauline sent this, she says they going to lynch her son born 21 years ago, mind you say twenty one years ago—then say—listen close—look in his eyes—and you'll save him. (50)

No one is certain of her motivations behind her action, but she does save her son. He escapes tragedy because of his progenitor.

Unfortunately, Johnson does not further explain the circumstances under which Jack came to be born. Pauline was married at the time, and it is unclear whether she was raped. It is likely, though, that this was indeed the case. Her husband has died, and although he raised Jack as his own son, it is possible he was aware of the situation. This was a common situation, particularly where the white perpetrator of the crime was in a position of power. Because Tinkhem is now governor, and at the time of the incident was most likely a white man with some status, there would have been no possibility of charging him with rape, or of confronting him about his fathering the child. Pauline's husband would have had little option except to accept the child as his own.

Absent from this portrayal are some of the elements seen in white-authored texts about racial mixing. Although Jack is said to be very attractive, Johnson has not created him as a very light-skinned person. He is also not looking "above his station." The whites in the community are all too eager to lynch him. He poses a threat to them because even modest aspirations were unacceptable in a young black man. Blacks in the community do not defer to him as though he were somehow "better" than they were. He does not aspire to whiteness or white privilege, nor does he attempt to deny his blackness. His ability to avert the impending tragedy is due to the seeming lack of attention he pays to his own skin color. He is not attempting to "pass."

Skin color plays a large part in Zora Neale Hurston's *Color Struck* (1925), but it is not the light-skinned character who is the tragic heroine in this play. One of Hurston's longer plays, *Color Struck* dramatizes the detrimental effects of miscegenation on the black community. Here the tragedy is again not centered on the children of miscegenation, but instead on those who identify light skin with privilege, and the consequences of the intraracial hatred that can emerge because of it.

Those with lighter skin are perceived to have more political and economic power, whether or not they actually have that power. More important to Hurston's dark-skinned character Emmaline, those who are light are deemed more beautiful. Emmaline's perspective demonstrates the degree to which some African Americans imposed white standards of beauty on themselves. In their eyes, the beautiful women were white or had white features. For black women, the equation of beauty and whiteness (or white features) has long been an issue of controversy, often to the detriment of community building and maintenance. As Hurston writes in *Dust Tracks on a Road*, "If it was so honorable and glorious to be black, why was it the yellow-skinned people among us had so much prestige? Even a child in the first grade could see that this was so from what happened in the classroom and on school programs" (1942: 234).

This controversy fuels Emmaline's hatred of herself and other black women, and her envy of those with light skin. She has become complicit in an antiblack mind-set that privileges whiteness. Her envy of light skin and hatred of darkness become her tragedy, not once but three times. She thus determines her tragic fate, while believing that it is determined by a "natural" law that is really a myth. The first time, she is on her way to a cakewalk with her dance partner and fiancé, John. Hurston describes John as "a light brown skinned man" (Perkins 1989: 89). Emma argues with John about his flirtations with a mulatta, Effie; she is convinced that John prefers Effie because of her complexion. In her rage, Emma breaks their engagement, and John goes on to win the cakewalk, with Effie. John's reasoning is that they wanted their town to win, but Emma can only see what she concludes are his attentions to Effie. "Oh, them half whites, they gets everything, they gets everything everybody else wants! The men, the jobs—everything!" (97). While her assessment of the advantages of being light skinned in a racist society is on target, her hatred has blinded her to John's professions of love. John and Effie win the cakewalk, and Emma leaves angry.

In the fourth scene of the play, we see Emma in her house

years later, and are aware of a child in the next room. Emma is reluctant to help, denying the child water. There is a knock on the door, and it is John, looking for Emma. We find that she is unmarried, and after much explaining, John nearly convinces Emma that he has always been in love with her. When she assumes that he married a light-skinned woman, John counters, "Naw she wasn't [high-yaller] neither. She was jus' as much like you as Ah could get her" (99). She is nearly convinced. When John realizes that her daughter is there, he is willing to take the child in as his own, but is surprised when he sees that she is very light skinned. When he asks her about it, Emma replies that she wasn't married, and the questions end there.

John is enthusiastic about getting a doctor for the child, and Emma hesitates. Once again, her hatred of light-skinned women distorts her perception of reality, and she convinces herself that John cares more about her daughter than he does about her. He sends her for the doctor, and she pretends to go, but instead waits and returns to surprise him sitting next to the girl. She is furious to see him sitting where she assumed he would be, and an argument ensues. John realizes that Emma hasn't changed in all of the time that has passed.

> So this is the woman I've been wearing over my heart like a rose for twenty years! She so despises her own skin that she can't believe anyone else could love it! Twenty years! Twenty years of adoration, of hunger, of worship! (On the verge of tears he crosses to door and exits quietly, closing the door after him.) (102)

For the second time, Emma loses the man she loves because she believes that he could not love her because of her skin. Emma's third tragedy is the death of her daughter. After John leaves, the doctor arrives, but it is too late. The play closes with the image of Emma sitting, rocking, and sobbing for the world she has lost. While Emma has spent her life hating the privilege she believes to be that of the mulatta, she has let her own chance for happiness escape.

We cannot be certain that Emma's views are irrational, however. For a woman in Emma's position, it is easy to see that within the American context, African Americans who *look* mixed, who show their "white blood," are much more likely to be well educated and middle class. Hurston advocates, here as well as in other places, that the problem for blacks in America is not themselves or their own communities, but the influence of whites and racism upon them. Hurston is an idealist; in her ideal world, Emma and John would have been able to be happy together, because the outside influence that gives privilege to individuals based on skin color would not have been a factor. Without the racist context of America, Emma would have had no reason to hate herself and her blackness. John would also have been unaffected. While John's words proclaim his love for Emma and his love for her blackness, his actions when he is with her only affirm her fears. In both of the scenes when John is given the opportunity to demonstrate to Emma that he does not privilege whiteness, he chooses it anyway. Hurston does not make either of the choices easy (winning the cakewalk or Emma; the life of the child or Emma). Emma does give him a chance to prove that she is wrong about him. In her eyes, and perhaps in ours as well, he fails both tests. He might have been able to prove his assertions with a picture of the woman he married, but he never shows Emma the picture.

Another of Hurston's plays, *Polk County* (never produced or published), also treats the issue of intraracial conflict, although that is not the central issue of the play. Hurston wrote the play with Dorothy Waring, and based it on her own experiences gathering folk materials in the South. It follows Hurston's folk aesthetic, creating a drama that depicts the lives of the poorest of Southern blacks. *Polk County* takes place in a sawmill camp, where most of the inhabitants are either the men who work there or their girl-friends, wives, or camp followers. In the introductory notes on the play, Hurston describes the women as "misfits from the outside.

67

Seldom good looking, intelligent, or adjustable. They had drifted down to their level, unable to meet the competition outside. Many have made time in prisons also. Usually for fighting over men" (Prologue 2–3).

Early in the play, conflict arises between Big Sweet and Dicey. Big Sweet, according to Hurston, is "a handsome negro woman around thirty. Physically very strong. She has a quick temper and great courage, but is generous and kind, and loyal to her friends. Has the quality of leadership" (Prologue 3). Dicey, on the other hand, is

> a homely narrow-contracted little black woman, who has been slighted by nature and feels "evil" about it. Suffers from the "black ass." Her strongest emotion is envy. What she passes off as deep love is merely the determination not to be outdone by handsomer women. Yearns to gain a reputation as "bad" (the fame of a sawmillcamp) to compensate her for her lack of success with men. [Because Dicey is] short, scrawny, and black, a pretty yellow girl arouses violent envy in her. (Prologue 3)

Dicey's complicity with white standards of female beauty are strengthened by her complicity within the patriarchal system. Instead of becoming part of the women's community, she has focused on competing with other women.

Eventually, a "pretty yellow girl," Leafy, does enter the sawmill camp, and Dicey leaves and plots revenge on the mulatta who she feels stole her man. The other women of the sawmill camp accept Leafy into their community, and she becomes Dicey's alleged rival for My Honey's affections. Leafy is at the camp to learn to sing the Blues, and Dicey is shamed away from the camp after trying to start a fight with Big Sweet, who has become Leafy's protector. Dicey has an entire scene to herself, where she laments the position in which her color places her. Like Emma in *Color Struck*, she is convinced that light-skinned women get whatever they want. Her efforts to get revenge against Big Sweet are in vain, and even the assistance of a local voodoo priestess cannot get her what she wants. In her solo scene, Dicey claims, "And these mens is so crazy! They aint got no sense. Always pulling after hair and looks. And these womens that got it is so grasping, and griping, and mean. They wants EVERYTHING—and they gits it too. Look like they would be satisfied with *some*. Naw, they wants it all" (Act 3, Scene 1, 2–3).

Hurston rarely has her characters encounter whites; instead, she portrays the lives of blacks within their own community. As Cheryl Wall asserts:

> Because [Hurston's] focus was on black cultural traditions, she rarely explored interracial themes [directly]. The black/white conflict, which loomed paramount in the fiction of her black contemporaries, in Wright's novels especially, hardly surfaced in Hurston's. . . . June Jordan has described how the absence of explicitly political protest caused Hurston's work to be devalued. Affirmation, not protest, is Hurston's hallmark. Yet, as Jordan argues, "affirmation of black values and lifestyle within the American context is, indeed, an act of protest." (1993: 77)

Leafy is particularly not tragic. Emma's daughter is tragic, but in a way that is profoundly different from the tragic mulatta of the white imagination. Her mother's hatred for her is responsible for her death, and she is not a character with whom we have a connection. We may not be able to use the word "tragedy," at least not in the classical sense, in Hurston's work at all. Her plays do not follow that standard structure, and the problems that face all the women—mulatta and otherwise—are really derived from the social structure of the United States, and the racism implicit in it. The women who place themselves on the outside, competing with other women, are those who have the most difficult lives. Those women who find community, especially when they are not involved in self-hatred, are the ones who escape tragedy.

For Hurston, then, the tragedy for the mulatta is societal, for it is the internalization of and complicity with the myths of white society that lead to tragic circumstances. While the women of the sawmill camp accept Leafy, Dicey does not; at the conclusion of the play, Leafy and My Honey are married, and Dicey leaves in shame. The tragedy here is Dicey's complicity with the standards established by the dominant culture, which uses color and race as guidelines for the distribution of power and wealth. As Hurston wrote in her autobiography, "the Negro race was not one band of heavenly love. There was stress and strain inside as well as out. Being black was not enough. It took more than a community of skin color to make your love come down on you" (1942: 242–43). Hurston did not believe in integration; she felt that "for everything put up in the South for white people there is the equivalent for the Negro. In other words, the Jim Crow system works. I feel that this is all right. After all, what Negroes need, and this is a principal factor in the race question, are just and equal opportunity. I don't mind dining with myself or with my people. In fact I should prefer to. And it works both ways" (quoted in Gilbert 1943). In theory, her response is legitimate, and Hurston privileged the theoretical. We know that while Hurston's personal situation growing up in the South may have made it seem that "separate but equal" was effective, for the vast majority of blacks in the South that was simply not true. In the 1940s, Hurston's opposition to integration seems consistent with Du Bois's perspective during the same period, although Du Bois was opposed to integration for its own sake (for integration to be the goal rather than a step toward ending racism). The influence of white culture and values would dilute the sense of community that existed in the black Southern towns Hurston knew.

Some of the characters constructed by the dominant culture appear to coincide with Hurston's perspective. Films such as Elia Kazan's *Pinky* reinforce the idea that the mulatta is best off when she remains within black culture, not for the sake of her history or culture, but so that she will not transgress into white society. African American writers supported the inclusion of those of mixed race, especially as their increased access to power could strengthen

black communities with access to higher education. *Pinky* con-
structs a mulatta whose life will be tragic if she does not conform
to the expectations of the dominant culture. We can see that the
three mulatta types written by whites during the same period are
different from those created in the plays by both Johnson and Hurston, where the tragedy of the mulatta is an external one, created
by the white supremacist culture.

What's Tragic about the Tragic Mulatta?   *read ???*

We have seen a variety of characters presented as tragic mulattas. Why tragic? What is it about tragedy that marks these women?
The use of the word "tragic" to describe these women necessitates
an analysis of the meaning of "tragedy" in this sense. While the
plays and films themselves are not tragedies (they are, overwhelm-
ingly, musicals and melodramas), the *characters* are tragic. They
must then have some of the qualities of tragedy to qualify as tragic,
and as we will see, many do.

If we look at tragedy in the classical Greek sense, then Zoe, to
be a tragic character, should have some hamartia, either an error
in judgment or a mistaken assumption. Zoe's hamartia lies in her
mistaken assumptions that she is free (that, in a twist, is not truly
in error, but for the purposes of the play, she does assume freedom
without having secure knowledge of it) and that George not only
knew about her heritage, but was also aware of the anti-miscegena-
tion laws in Louisiana. Recognition, reversal, and a cathartic event
are also evident in this script, lending to its "tragic" nature. The
recognition comes in the revelation to George of Zoe's race; the
reversal comes at the point at which Zoe's fortunes are reversed,
i.e., when she is told that she is not really free.

Even more important for the element of tragedy, Zoe represents a contagion, a threat to the community, and she must be sac-
rificed for that transgression. Here lies the cathartic event in *The
Octoroon*, where the offender either dies or is exiled. When the

71

mulatta seeks to step outside her prescribed arena, she threatens boundaries and cannot be allowed to live. What Zoe's death ultimately accomplishes is the restoration of the community. George can go on to marry someone else, because the debt has been cleared and the plantation is his, free and clear. In addition, Zoe's mixed status makes George's desire for her dangerous for two reasons. First, part of the mythology of the mulatta is that, being the offspring of two different races (like the mule, for whom she is named), she must be sterile. Were George and Zoe to marry, they might never have children. Second, if Zoe does have children, they would technically be "black," because only one drop of "black blood" is necessary to make the "Negro." In the American context, Zoe is the sacrificial victim who absolves the political state; she provides the group catharsis, for the audience and also for the other characters in the play. This is particular to the American context; as has been documented, the play's ending was revised for its London premiere. Peter Thompson (1984) claims, in the collection of Boucicault's plays that he edited, that the London ending was changed because the audience wanted a happy ending or because the original was too complicated. While Boucicault's original revision is no longer extant, a review provides a summary of the concluding act:

> Ultimately he [M'Closky] is chased through the Red Cedar Swamp to the Painted Rocks, where he maintains his position from a rocky ledge against his assailants, having possessed himself of a gun with six charges, until he is brought down by a shot from George Peyton; Salem Scudder, by an act of self-sacrifice, having occasioned him to expose his body to Peyton's aim. The fair Octoroon is thus set at liberty; and the piece concludes with a declaration that in another land Zoe and Peyton will solemnize a lawful union, and live for the happiness of each other. (Quoted in Thompson 1984: 225)

The question remains: was the ending changed to appease a London audience that wanted a happy ending, or was Boucicault following what he by then understood as the particularly American dilemma of mixed race when he wrote the original ending? Still, whether Zoe dies or simply leaves to marry George elsewhere, the play ends in a standard catharsis (their departure amounts to exile for Zoe). I argue that the tragic Octoroon (in this instance) is a particularly American phenomenon, and her fate (in America) must be appropriately tragic.

Pinky's hamartia lies in her belief that she can live her life as white without consequences, and she attempts to remain unshaken in this belief through most of the film. Her belief, that might well be an example of Sartrean bad faith, becomes untenable once she must admit publicly (and in a nationally public way) that she is not the person she has been claiming to be. Her recognition scene is one that is forced upon her in a way that will characterize the films of this period. The public revelation of her origins makes passing virtually impossible. She does not have to sacrifice her life, however. Because she decides against her marriage to her white fiancé, catharsis can be satisfied with simple exile. In this case, she even enjoys her exile—life as a black woman in the South. Thus both *Pinky* and *The Octoroon* demonstrate elements of classical tragedy not in genre but in character.

Contemporary Mulattas and the Tragic Myth

In the 1960s, at the peak of the civil rights movement and at a time when even light-skinned blacks were exploring the beauty of blackness and identifying solely with their African heritage, Adrienne Kennedy was exploring her racially mixed heritage on the stage. Her first play, *Funnyhouse of a Negro*, was written in 1961 and first produced in 1964, the same year that LeRoi Jones's *Dutchman* premiered. Kennedy reinvented the tragic mulatta, and explores what may be the true tragedy of the mulatta. The tragedy stems from the place that her character, Sarah, must occupy within white American culture.

Funnyhouse of a Negro centers around Sarah, an African American woman who is the daughter of a dark-skinned man and a white-looking mother. She is losing touch with any coherent or whole self, and she splits her consciousness into five parts. One, which is herself in the life she leads, is hiding from the African part of her heritage, and instead has surrounded herself with whites, when she has not shut herself away in her apartment. Even her apartment is filled with the symbols of white American and European culture. Her other selves are the Duchess of Hapsburg, Queen Victoria, Jesus, and Patrice Lumumba.

Sarah's disjuncture stems from her self-hatred and from hatred of things black. Whiteness and the symbols of white culture, like the bust of Queen Victoria that she keeps in her room, are the things with which she fills her life. She has learned from American culture that whiteness is to be valued, as are items from white European culture. Conscious of the fact that white skin is valued over black skin, Sarah knows that she might have been "white" if her mother had not married the blackest man around. The character Sarah searches for her own identity, attempting to deal with her double life and her split selves. As a child of mixed blood, a whole or unified self would include both African and European heritage; unfortunately, her culture will not allow her to claim both sides of her heritage. Because she is the product of a nearly white woman and a black Christian missionary, the parts of her psyche that occupy one side or the other of the dichotomy create a conflict within her. The duchess and Queen Victoria fight against the martyred African savior/liberator, Patrice Lumumba, and Jesus, leaving no space for reconciliation, recognition, or spiritual wholeness. Those who run the Funnyhouse, Raymond and the Landlady, the Funnyman and Funnywoman, respectively, do not allow Sarah to identify herself, and laugh at the crisis they observe within her. The only way out for Sarah is suicide, to quiet the fighting between the two parts of her life that cannot be reconciled.

Kennedy attempts to portray an African American woman

who is plagued by issues of self and identity. Sarah says in one monologue,

> Victoria always wants me to tell her of whiteness. She wants me to tell her of a royal world where everything and everyone is white and there are no unfortunate black ones. For as we of royal blood know, black is evil and has been from the beginning. (1988: 5)

Sarah has learned to hate her blackness, influenced by her education and a society that hates blackness. She is proud of her features, which do not identify her as black, but hates the hair that does identify her race, and that falls out more and more as the play progresses. Sarah's self-hatred seems rooted in the images of blackness that dominate her culture. She wants to lose any remaining racial markers, and become pallid like Negroes on the covers of American Negro magazines; soulless, educated, and irreligious" (5). She counts on her friends, her antiques, and her bust of Queen Victoria to help her escape any sense of her race; they are her insulation. For, like all educated Negroes—out of life and death essential—I find it necessary to maintain a stark fortress against recognition of myself" (6). Despite her self-denial, both of the figures of the dominant culture—Raymond and the Landlady—view Sarah as black. She is trapped by the powerful icon of the mulatta.

Those of Sarah's selves who are manifestations of Western colonialism and antiblack racism spout stereotypes about blacks, especially about black men and their allegedly rampant sexuality. The Duchess of Hapsburg describes Sarah's father in terms which reveal her colonialist thinking. He is referred to as African, despite American origins; "jungle," "nigger," and "missionary" invoke iconic Africa. Sarah claims that her father raped her mother, further drawing on the stereotyped image of the black male. Sarah's father forced his blackness on her mother, causing her mother's hair to fall out. Sarah's being forced to accept the half of her that is not white causes her to lose her hair as well. Sarah's mother had hair, skin, and eyes that could be seen as "white." However Sarah might identify with these white (or white-looking) females, she also has one particular self—Patrice Lumumba—that identifies strongly with what is most feared by the duchess and Queen Victoria.

In Patrice Lumumba, Sarah connects with her race via one of the most famous African revolutionaries (1925–61, prime minister of the Republic of the Congo). She has chosen this self to be represented by an African man, one who led a revolution against a colonial power. In this guise, Sarah is a black revolutionary. The monologue of Lumumba presents an altered view of Sarah's father, and contrasts sharply with the view of the duchess. Sarah/Lumumba remembers her father:

> [He] pleaded with me to help him find Genesis, search for Genesis in the midst of golden savannas, nim and white franko-penny trees and white stallions roaming under a blue sky, help him search for the white doves, he wanted the black man to make a pure statement, he wanted the black man to rise from colonialism. (14)

Although the vision of Africa is that of a Christian paradise, the call for revolution is clear. Sarah, under the influence of Lumumba, does not see her father as the bestial jungle inhabitant, but instead as human, and sees him aspiring for something more. Other than Sarah's primary self, this is the only other black self. Her primary black female self must find its way with no help from anyone else, her mother was too close to being white, her father was too black (and male) to be a model for her. In addition, Sarah's identification with the savior figures connects to an historical role of the light skinned: Savior of the Race.

Depending on the moment, Sarah may see herself reflected as any one of these, or as all of them. Ultimately, what is present in the person of Sarah (and her selves) is the confusion of the Other who cannot find her self represented anywhere. Sarah's experience is based on these figures. Her only history is a collection of myth and mythologized figures. Despite the existence of her parents, and knowledge of her paternal grandmother, she does not draw coherence or strength from any of these figures. She has no ancestral ties to which she can directly relate.

There are similar resonances in Kennedy's second play, *The Owl Answers* (1965). She retains the multiplicities she used in *Funnyhouse*, although they are used in a different way. The protagonist of the play is "She who is Clara Passmore [who cannot pass, and is seen as black] who is the Virgin Mary who is the Bastard who is the Owl" (25); this time, each of the character's selves are included in one body. Clara is not the only character to have more than one identity; her mother is "Bastard's Black Mother who is the Reverend's Wife who is Anne Boleyn," and her father is "Goddam Father who is the Richest White Man in the Town who is Reverend Passmore" (25). Kennedy has each of them retain some part of their costume from the character; thus the audience visually connects the characters played by the same actor. Again, Kennedy uses four historical/mythical figures who intrude on Clara's world: William Shakespeare, William the Conqueror, Geoffrey Chaucer, and Anne Boleyn. Like Sarah's other selves, these figures serve to torture Clara, although they do not represent parts of her self. As in the final group scene in *Funnyhouse*, the voices speak in ensemble. They do not have individual lines, but speak as a single voice of England, Western civilization, and white America.

Their project is to keep Clara from seeing her father, who is buried in the Tower of London. According to them, she is a Negro; they call her his ancestor, and declare that an impossibility. Clara is the daughter of the Richest White Man in the Town and the woman who cooked for him; in this Kennedy is drawing on the historical references of black women. Clara's history is a tangle of her father and mother, her adoptive parents, the Reverend Passmore and his wife, and those who are her ancestors (or the ones whose ancestor she is, for the text calls her their ancestor), the figures of colonial power of England. Clara's seeking involves not only the burial of her father at St. Paul's Cathedral, but also her exploring London with him, praying with the reverend's wife, and looking for black men on the subway to take to a hotel room in Harlem.

Clara says that "Bastard they say, the people in the town all say Bastard, but I—I belong to God and the owls, ow, and I sat in the fig tree" (35). Kennedy herself felt that she existed between and within two cultures; in *People Who Led To My Plays*, she explains that

> I'd often stare at the statue of Beethoven I kept on the left-hand side of my desk. I felt it contained a "secret." I'd do the same with the photograph of Queen Hatshepsut that was on the wall. I did *not* then understand that I felt torn between these forces of my ancestry . . . European and African . . . a fact that would one day explode in my work. (1989: 96)

Clara's position is like Sarah's; they occupy a space that is the site of a confluence of cultures—African, African American, and European—which leaves them no solid ground on which to stand. They are all of these identities, but they are not rooted in any of them. This place of confluence is the tragedy of the mulatta, for she is part of more than one culture in a society that requires that she occupy only one. Clara expresses the silent suffering of those who must live with the fact that their fathers were their mothers' masters. This is not to say that Sarah or Clara should no longer identify herself as black, nor does it deny that, in essence, to be black in the United States is to be of mixed race. Instead, it accentuates the idea that how either of them self-identifies matters little in the larger culture. For Clara, those who guard European culture see her as a Negro, despite how she may see herself. Sarah's white boyfriend, Raymond, does not see the whiteness of Sarah's mother, he only sees her as the exotic "little liar" (*Funnyhouse* 23) whose father is black. Both Clara and Sarah are read as black through the eyes of the dominant culture.

This culture denies them the right to determine their identities, which is a white privilege. Being marked as "black," at least through Kennedy's eyes, is to be witness to a culture that will not allow you to exist within it. The old expectation that the mulatta or person of mixed race will remain entirely in the culture of black America places blacks in a difficult position. Despite their own mixed racial heritage, mulattas cannot be a part of the dominant culture, because that is defined around visible markers of race. At the same time, they are expected to exist in a culture within a culture, one that is marked as they are, inferior.

Of all the representations of persons of mixed race, Kennedy's tragic mulattas seem most to give a visual presentation and a human figure to W. E. B. Du Bois's concept of the "seventh son" that he presents in *The Souls of Black Folk*:

> It is a peculiar sensation, this double-consciousness, this sense of always looking at one's self through the eyes of others, of measuring one's soul by the tape of a world that looks on in amused contempt and pity. One ever feels his two-ness,—an American, a Negro; two souls, two thoughts, two unreconciled strivings; two warring ideals in one dark body, whose dogged strength alone keeps it from being torn asunder. (1929: 3–4)

Either one has the strength to attempt to keep one's self together, or one embodies the tragic mulatta, who like Sarah loses herself in madness, or like Sarah Jane and Julie, exists in torment. As Du Bois wrote, the life of the black in America, whether obviously mixed with white or not, is a constant struggle "to merge his double self into a better and truer self. In this merging he wishes neither of the older selves to be lost" (1929: 4). The tragedy is not the fault of the mulatta, or her parents, but in fact is pressed upon her by a culture that cannot allow her to exist as she is. In a society where the distribution of power is rooted in the reading of race, gender, and class, the mulatta is a threat. She is still a fascinating figure within the American cultural imagination, because "marking" attempts to separate people into distinct cultures.

79

Some of this attention is directed to the parents of mixed-race children; however, the racializing of the child is still very important. Two contemporary pop culture "mulattas," both in the music industry, demonstrate the contemporary American obsession with racializing. As Lisa Jones explores in an essay in *Bulletproof Diva* (1994), both Paula Abdul and Mariah Carey were of "questionable" racial heritage. Abdul, partially because of her "obvious" visual racial markers, ethnic-sounding last name, and association with black musicians, was marketed to dance music audiences, comprised largely of blacks. Carey was marketed to a more mixed pop audience, and record company executives worked hard to keep her parentage a secret. In fact, the companies hoped they would be able to market both women more broadly if they were *heard* to be "black" yet were *visually* presented as white; they could thus market both women to black and white audiences. While Abdul was not interested in keeping her parents in the closet, so to speak, Carey evaded questions and responded that her father was "Brazilian." Her own efforts to pass culminated in her thanking the black community for one of "their" awards at the NAACP Image Awards.

The differences between the two women show the extent to which racial identity remains crucial for some. It was not important to Abdul whether her audiences knew what her racial identity was; she was not attempting to pass for white. Why was it so important that they pass? Perhaps, despite the increasing number of interracial marriages and multiethnic children, it still matters how much, if any, of your blood is African, and how much you identify with blackness.

The "problem of the mulatto" remains with American culture to the present. However, perhaps it is more appropriate to say the problem of *race* remains with the culture, for it is certainly not the person of mixed race who is problematic, but the way in which racial categories have functioned as class symbols. In her 1986 play *Combination Skin*, Lisa Jones presents the contemporary tragic mulatta in the format of a game show—"The $100,000 Tragic Mulatto." There are three contestants, each of whom is guided into her unconscious to examine the depth of her mulattahood. For Jones, the degree to which any of them is a mulatta is based not on skin color or even background but on the extent to which each imagines herself as white. The three "specimens" each occupy a particular position, both consciously and unconsciously, on blackness and whiteness in America.

The text is rooted in the culture of the 1980s, and many of the references are time specific. Particularly, Jones draws on the "buppie" (black upwardly mobile) image, and the Reagan-era antiaffirmative action mind-set. Color is less important; Vendetta Goldwoman, the host of the show, says, "It's a wonderful moment to be born young, gifted, and half and half, or better yet, young, buxom, and white at heart" (1996: 220). In fact, in the social-climbing days of the 1980s, "You don't even have to be light or bright these days, just shed your skin, state your claim, your piece of the great white way" (220). We find that, in fact, the two physical mulattas are not the most tragic; that honor is reserved for the truly white at heart.

Specimen 1 is the wealthy mixed-race child from the predominantly white suburbs. She identifies herself as part of the human race, refusing to categorize herself as white or black. In her journey into her unconscious, she is honored for writing the "universal" novel *Combination Skin*, which is about *The* Black Experience. One element of the novel is that all of the "fair-skinned, wavy-haired young heroines in the book [are] always being deflowered by blue-black casanova kings of hoodoo" (221). Her unconscious, then, is obsessed with blackness and black experience.

Specimen 2 is even less the typical tragic mulatta; she has surrounded herself with black culture, despite the fact that she was born in Palo Alto to a Jewish mother who teaches "Hebrew Language and Literature" (224). As Vendetta says, she is an "honest to goodness young hybrid" (224); unlike the other two specimens, she is truly culturally as well as racially mixed. Having a Jewish mother makes her Jewish as well as black. She is defensively proud of her blackness, as opposed to Specimen 1 who simply fails to mention it. Specimen 2 says, "It's the whites that impose the blood question. Don't you understand, my fallen black queen? It's up to us, the African people, the chosen, to combat their propaganda" (225). Her deepest secret is that her father doesn't claim her. "You'll never be black," he says in her dream. "And you'll never know what it's like. Stop reading the books. Your blood's too thin" (226). This twist reverses what has been the standard; for her father, the "one drop" rule does not make her black.

Specimen 3 is from Detroit, presses her own hair, and wears an aromatherapy-type scent called "Mulatto"; "so sheer, yet so complex" (227). Her deepest, darkest secrets are anything but dark; in her unconscious, she dreams of a world where everyone and everything is white. One of her lovers is "the white supremacist [who] will be waiting in his white robe" (228). She wins, for in her unconscious, she is the most tragic mulatta.

Specimen 2's way of dealing with her existence within the culture is to identify with blackness. Specimen 1 prefers to live in a world where multicultural is assumed to mean antiracist, but it actually leaves her a way to avoid identifying herself as black. Specimen 3's lily-white imaginary world stands for the myth of America, where with the right dream and the right attitude, she can shed her blackness for white American-ness. Passing, in Jones's view, is no longer so strongly rooted in the visual but in the psychological. It is the same conclusion that Franz Fanon reached in his classic *Black Skin, White Masks* (1952). As with Paula Abdul and Mariah Carey, the visual is still the primary sign-system through which race is registered; however, the identification from the outside can remain valid only if the self-identification confirms it. Carey can be seen by her black audience as black, but she does not identify herself as black. Her self-identification attempts to deny the visual because, like Specimen 3, she sees herself as white. If she does not see herself as black, and refuses to be identified that way, then one community response to that is to "deny" her (many blacks now refuse to buy her records, prompting her to work with popular artists like Boyz II Men in hopes of reviving the market).

Ever finer racial distinctions appear in the American consciousness as reflected in the media, and the number of racial categories increases. These distinctions are a current cultural obsession. The cover of the February 13, 1995, edition of *Newsweek* asks, "What color is black?" Nine pages of the issue are devoted to questions of race. While the writers seem to understand that relations between blacks and whites are not nearly as good as they should be, they offer up multiracial categories as solutions to defeat racism. Another article in the section explores the scientific research that declares there are no genetic races, at least as can be derived from the Human Genome Diversity Project. If there are no genetic races, and people share attributes cross-racially, then all organization around race functions as a social construct. According to the article, those who wish to retain the outmoded categories of race are simply accepting the unfounded science of the nineteenth century.

The March 1995 issue of *Forbes American Heritage* magazine has an article written by Shirlee Taylor Haizlip, author of the book *The Sweeter the Juice*. It documents her search for a branch of her family tree that decided to pass as white. While she does not advocate forming new racial categories, Haizlip does claim that the races, as they are viewed, are not as "pure" as they appear to be.

With all of this, there is still the fact that race is not simply a matter of beauty or acceptance. It is also not only a question of biology or social construction. Whether race has always existed, or if it is only a creation of nineteenth-century science, the larger issue is that race and racial categories do exist now, and that those categories have become the basis for the distribution of power and wealth. However or whenever "socially constructed," racial identity also forms a base of shared history and culture, from which many of its members gain strength. The question of identity brings with it those of community, power, and politics, which function from community bases. American playwrights and screenwriters have been wrestling with the divisive issue of racial purity for more than a century without finding any solutions. Black playwrights claim those of mixed black-white ancestry as their own, perhaps because the latter were visually most easily categorized there, but essentially because they understand that *black* in the United States is already a category of mixture. Most American blacks can point to other races in their ancestry (Native American, European, Asian).

Also, as bell hooks claims, for those of mixed race to identify as black is a revolutionary act. Those who do so are resisting white supremacist thought and rejecting the "promise of mainstream success only if we are willing to negate the value of blackness" (hooks 1992: 17). It is a perspective assumed by writers like Georgia Douglas Johnson and Zora Neale Hurston. At the same time, mainstream culture is sending mixed messages. On the one hand, if you're even partially black, you should be in the black community. Trespass on white power and privilege, and you risk being miserable for the rest of your life. Views like this are expressed in the denial of Julie's character in *Show Boat* being a racist depiction. Besides, those who pass as white, and marry whites, pose a threat to the racial purity of future generations. On the other hand, there are a number of whites, particularly liberal whites and those who have mixed children, to create and support a mixed-race category. In both cases, blackness is recognized as being the least desirable.

Until power relations are no longer defined by racial difference, black and white American playwrights will not solve their ambivalence about those of mixed race. It is more than simplistic to create new categories; under apartheid in South Africa, having a class of mixed-race people did not lead to the abolition of racism. In fact, it created deeper rifts between people who might otherwise have been allies. The apartheid system still granted privilege on the basis of skin color and/or ancestry. In fact, the erection of more and finer racial and ethnic distinctions generates and legitimates racist practices. As long as racial difference is connected to power, the tragic mulatta will have a place on American stage and screen, as the 1994 revival of *Show Boat* evidences.

Chapter 3

The Myth of the Whore:

Jezebel and the Revision of Black Women's Sexuality

The jezebel is yet another image of black women created and disseminated by the dominant culture. Like the mammy and the tragic mulatta, this image is based in the imagination of antiblack racists; unlike the other two, the jezebel image was rooted in the discourse of science. She does not appear in American drama and film until the twentieth century, even though the centuries-old myth of the sexual nature of people of African descent was "justified" in the nineteenth century.

Jezebel is important because it is through this icon that the connections between sex, gender, race, and power most readily expose themselves. The racist and colonialist thinking that makes the situation of some of the children of interracial parentage difficult even in the late twentieth century is descended from beliefs about race, sexuality, and gender formulated in earlier centuries. As Patricia Hill Collins notes, "biological notions of race and gender prevalent in the early nineteenth century that fostered the animalistic icon of Black female sexuality were joined by the appearance of a racist biology incorporating the concept of degeneracy" (1990: 171). Actually, European and American biologists of the eighteenth and nineteenth centuries conceived of Africans as fundamentally different from the white race; in fact, Africans were viewed as a step up from apes, and thus more animal in nature. Fiction of the "dark continent" is replete with these images. Western biologists were fascinated with the sexual practice and sexual organs of blacks. The famous African woman Sarah Bartmann, alias the "Venus Hottentot," was kept as a specimen for public viewing while she was alive, and after her death, her genitalia were dissected and put on display.

The genitalia of blacks were deemed larger than the average for whites, a notion that led scientists to the conclusion that blacks must be much more sexually active, unrestrained, and even sexually aggressive. This "evidence" came from nineteenth-century Europeans, who invented the science of physiognomy in their search for a biological foundation for their beliefs that certain people were inherently "lower," i.e., closer to animals than others. Much of the research concentrated on "criminal" personalities, which included prostitutes, mannish women, and non-white women. Bartmann and other African women were discovered to have physically different genitalia. In Bartmann's case, this was due to the tribal practice of lengthening the labia. In her culture this was a mark of beauty, but Europeans viewed these physical anomalies to be natural in blacks, and thought that Bartmann's genitalia were "deformed" from birth. Connections were also made between blacks and apes, unfortunately furthered by Charles Darwin's theory of evolution. The alleged similarities between them became scientific evidence of the inferiority of blacks.

Biology's "scientific" exploration of the sexuality of black women did not stop with exoticization. Theodor Billroth, in 1877, claimed that the overdevelopment of the clitoris, which he associated with the "Hottentot apron," led to lesbianism. It was also found that white prostitutes eventually acquired similarly enlarged labia, but prostitutes' labia were enlarged mainly due to tumors from venereal diseases acquired in their profession (Gilman 1985a: 223). It was also claimed that white prostitutes became increasingly masculine as they aged; the enlarged clitoris was a sign of deviant sexuality and lesbianism. Through this web of associations,

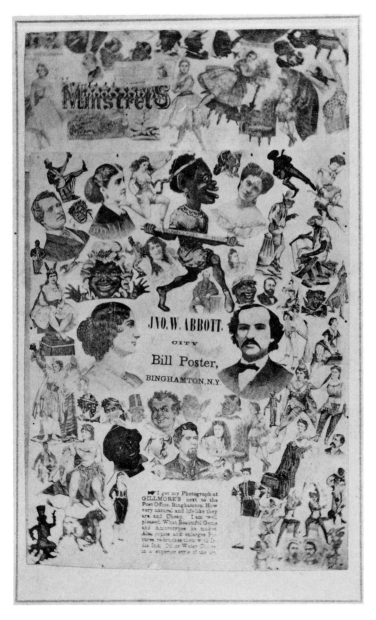

Poster with minstrel characters. Courtesy of Billy Rose Theatre Collection, New York Public Library.

The Mammy is
appalled at the
Northern servant's
behavior, *The
Birth of a Nation*
(1915). Courtesy
of the Film Stills
Archive, Museum
of Modern Art.

Mammy tries to help the family survive after the Civil War in
Gone With the Wind (1939). Courtesy of the Film Stills Archive,
Museum of Modern Art.

Delilah, in her mammy costume, *Imitation of Life* (1934). Courtesy of the Film Stills Archive, Museum of Modern Art.

Ruth and Travis watch Mama open the envelope in the Seattle
Group Theatre's 1994 production of *A Raisin in the Sun*.
Courtesy of the Seattle Group Theatre.

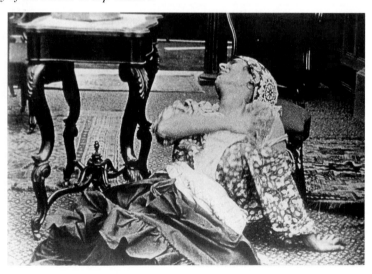

Stonewall's mulatta servant tears at her clothes, *The Birth of a Nation*
(1915). Courtesy of the Film Stills Archive, Museum of Modern Art.

The young black doctor tries to convince Pinky to open a nursing school, *Pinky* (1949). Courtesy of the Film Stills Archive, Museum of Modern Art.

Julie sings her last song in the Trocadero, *Show Boat* (1936). Courtesy of the Film Stills Archive, Museum of Modern Art.

Joe attempts to subdue Carmen, *Carmen Jones* (1954). Courtesy of the Film Stills Archive, Museum of Modern Art.

Sara Jane performs a table dance, *Imitation of Life* (1959). Courtesy of the Film Stills Archive, Museum of Modern Art.

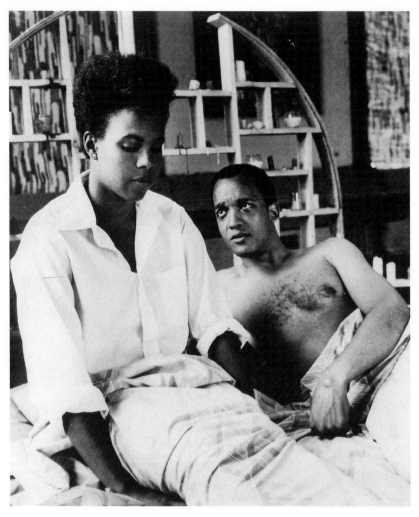

Nola and Jamie in Nola's bed-shrine, *She's Gotta Have It* (1984). Courtesy of the Films Stills Archive, Museum of Modern Art.

then, black women were linked with prostitution, sexual excess, deviancy, and lesbianism. Blacks, viewed as inherently sexual creatures, were believed to sexualize the environment and society they occupied.

During slavery, blacks were treated like animals, mated for the most promising offspring. The myth of black female sexuality provided an opportunity for white males to own women who would then be available to them sexually. Nineteenth-century white women were invested in the "cult of true womanhood"; they were to keep themselves chaste and not work outside the home. Black women, who could not be "true women" because of their status, provided a sexual outlet for white slave owners. According to Collins, "Black 'whores' made white 'virgins' possible. . . . The sexually denigrated woman . . . could be used as the yardstick against which the cult of true womanhood was measured" (1990: 176). White women were taught to submit to sex, which was linked to the duty of procreation rather than the pleasure of sexuality.

The myth of black women's aggressive sexuality had been formulated earlier; during the late nineteenth and early twentieth centuries, middle-class, educated black women strove to counter this myth by presenting themselves to society as chaste and moral. However, the jezebel icon was already too familiar to Americans; as Collins says, "Jezebel's function was to relegate all Black women to the category of sexually aggressive women, thus providing a powerful rationale for the widespread sexual assaults by white men typically reported by Black slave women" (177). The Old Testament Jezebel was a Phoenician princess who worshiped the god Baal. Temple prostitution was an element of the followers of Baal; in addition, Jezebel was responsible for the exiling of the Hebrew prophet Elijah (1 Kings). The association of the biblical Jezebel with prostitution and defying moral authority led to the iconization of Jezebel in Christianity, and thus the icon found its way into African American culture.

Not only did the jezebel icon present black women as sexually aggressive, but the values inherent in the characterization of blacks as uninhibitedly sexual also would lay the foundations for the later notion that blacks were amoral. This mythology rested on the belief that blacks were fundamentally biologically different from whites, and were not part of the human species; "human" meant "white." Although blacks were not in fact sexually or otherwise physiologically different—"deviant"—from whites, they were thought to be so. According to the logic of the myth, the deviancy and amorality of blacks led them to have children out of wedlock, contributing to the poverty and crime in black communities.

The sexual black woman is deemed dangerous because she appears capable of undermining the patriarchal notions of family on which the country was based. Her self-sufficiency makes it seem that her only need for men must be sexual. She is also envisioned as a destroyer of black men and manhood, which she accomplishes by pulling black men down from their "proper" role as patriarch within the family. Daniel Patrick Moynihan's welfare mother of the 1960s, or Newt Gingrich's of the 1990s, is a contemporary jezebel image of a black woman who cannot control herself, continues to have children without being married, and relies on others to support them. This is still the old myth of the jezebel, dressed up in both liberal concern and conservative disgust. This "natural" deviance of blacks not only supports white privilege but also argues that blacks are inherently unable to adapt to white mores. The myths support each other; blacks are in a catch-22. They are believed deviant because their families are socially abnormal; their families are allegedly abnormal because blacks have an uncontrolled biological sexual urge that renders them incapable of settling into the patriarchal family mode.

Jezebel's threat is not restricted to the larger structures of family and nation. She can also independently be the source of destruction of herself and of the men who become involved with her. Jezebel's image is like that of the black widow spider that kills the male when she has finished mating with him, or the *vagina dentata* that consumes the male after sex. The animal metaphors resurface; the jezebel is represented as a tiger, a puma, a panther, or other large, sleek cat who slinks up and pounces on her prey. She is a frightening apparition in the white imagination; she has been frequently represented thus in American culture.

Sex, Sexuality, and Black Women: The Insatiable and Dangerous

The icon of the jezebel contains several different meanings. Sometimes the jezebel represents dangerous sex; falling prey to her charms means trouble to her and her male victim. Usually, the man's inability to resist her brings her downfall as well as his. In other cases, jezebel is embodied by the light-skinned woman who attempts to pass for white; her primary outlet for success is the sex trade. This aspect of the jezebel ties into the tragic mulatta icon; her hidden blackness makes her sexually attractive, as we see in the case of Zoe in *The Octoroon*. She thus is a perfect candidate for sex work. Sometimes the jezebel expresses sexual availability; she behaves as though her primary need in life is sex, and that need must be fulfilled above all others. She is the "super-freak," to quote singer Rick James, or the nymphomaniac. There have been some of every variety in American theatre and film during the twentieth century.

The folk opera *Porgy and Bess* premiered in 1935, effectively broadening the audience for the first jezebel we will examine, Bess. *Porgy and Bess* was an adaptation of Dorothy and DuBose Heyward's play *Porgy*, which was one of those plays about blacks written by whites, allegedly treating them realistically. *Porgy* premiered in New York in 1924, and both it and *Porgy and Bess*, like other plays written for blacks during this period (Eugene O'Neill's *The Emperor Jones*, Marc Connelly's *The Green Pastures*, and Paul Greene's *In Abraham's Bosom*, for example), show the base side of the lives of African Americans. While Catfish Row may have verisimilitude, placing it on stage without contrasting images creates a myth. There was a real Catfish Row in Charleston, South

Carolina, and a real Porgy. The real Porgy was not the hero the Heywards created; he was considered to be a public nuisance.

The play and folk opera take place in Catfish Row, a poor black neighborhood in Charleston. Porgy is a beggar, a gambler, and a cripple. Though addicted to gambling, he does seem to make enough money, between begging and the goat he owns, to live fairly comfortably. It is rumored that he is "sof' on" Bess, the girlfriend of the murderer Crown (Heyward 1959: 215). Maria, the neighborhood matriarch, calls Bess a "licker-guzzlin' slut" (215), giving the audience a valuable clue to Bess's character. A group of men, including Crown, Sportin' Life, and Porgy, gathers to shoot craps. Bess is there, and before long Sportin' Life is handing out his "happy dust." While the group gambles, a fight breaks out and Crown kills one of them. Crown leaves town quickly to avoid prosecution, and Bess decides that Porgy will be her best protection.

Bess soon moves in with Porgy, becoming "his woman." She seems to be reforming herself, and their relationship is supportive. Porgy even buys a divorce for Bess from Crown. But things are not all rosy, and soon afterward a buzzard tries to land on their house. As Porgy says, "Once de buzzard fold he wing an' light over yo' do, yo' know all yo' happiness done dead" (244). The buzzard doesn't land, but it does signal the point from which things begin to go downhill. Bess goes off to the picnic with the others, and the buzzard takes the opportunity to light atop Porgy's door; he is unable to scare it away. While at the picnic, Bess meets up with Crown.

Because of her wild nature, Bess can't resist going back to Crown, who has decided that he will return and claim Bess once the cotton season has ended. Porgy is aware of their meeting, and Bess admits that she cannot resist Crown. Porgy vows to keep Crown away from her; he is helped by a hurricane that leaves a young child orphaned. Bess takes the child in, and for a while has a respectable life with Porgy. Their happy life is doomed to failure; when Crown returns to claim Bess, he is killed by Porgy, who ends up in jail after he is summoned to identify Crown. When Porgy returns after a few unexpected years in jail, Bess has left again, this time with Sportin' Life; the two of them have caught a boat to New York City. The sexual relationship between Bess and Porgy is downplayed; unlike Crown, Porgy is attempting to live as a moral citizen, which includes eschewing blatant sexuality.

Bess's amorality includes both an unrestrained sexuality and a desire for drugs and trouble, and her amorality leads to the destruction of Porgy's dream. Not even the things that should convince her to leave her old life behind—a good man and a child—are effective. Bess is at home in the juke joints of the poorest Southern blacks; it was to such depictions of black life that W. E. B. Du Bois objected. The Heywards were the authors of another play concerning the lower classes of blacks in South Carolina; *Mamba's Daughters* (1929) includes the character Hagar, a violent and sexual black woman. She is also ignorant. Her daughter, Lissa, is "naturally" different; very light skinned (she was played by Fredi Washington in the film version), she goes on to become a successful singer in New York. Lissa very nearly falls from grace, but instead of actively seeking destruction, she is assaulted.

The decades that followed *Porgy and Bess* tended to reinforce the views of blacks as amoral, violent, and aggressively sexual. In 1944, Oscar Hammerstein II's *Carmen Jones* appeared on the Broadway stage. It was an adaptation of Bizet's *Carmen*, transferred to a black American community during World War II. Of course, there was no better place to situate a story like *Carmen* in America; the dominant image of black Americans could much more easily accommodate the transferral. There is Carmen, the bad sexual woman; Joe, a brave but misguided soldier; Husky, as a boxer, replaces the bullfighter. Hammerstein himself states in his introduction that "the nearest thing in our modern American life to an equivalent of the gypsies in Spain is the Negro. Like the gypsy, he expresses his feelings simply, honestly, and graphically. Also as with the gypsy there is rhythm in his body, and music in his heart" (1945: xviii). Hammerstein's picture of the black soldier contradicts the actual valor and service of black soldiers during World War II.

91

Carmen Jones does follow the original opera, although Hammerstein adjusts it enough that it is instead a musical. At the beginning of the musical, Joe, the soldier, is visited by his sweetheart, Cindy Lou, but apparently Carmen has her eye on him. In her first song, Carmen lays her cards on the table:

> You go for me an' I'm taboo,
> But if yore hard to get I go for you
> An' if I do, den you are through, boy.
> My baby, dat's de end of you.
> De end of you. (Hammerstein 1945: 14)

"Dat's love," according to Carmen; her bad girl sexuality will seduce her man, but will destroy him in the end. We know that as much as Joe tries to remain faithful to Cindy Lou, he must eventually fall prey to Carmen's machinations.

Carmen shortly gets into a fight with another of the women working in the parachute factory, and Joe is the one who finds them fighting. Carmen's employment would also have been considered a threat during the period, and would not have been possible if it were not wartime. Because he stops Carmen, Joe is chosen to take her to the guardhouse. This falls in line with Carmen's devious plan, and while they are on their way to the guardhouse, she convinces him to set her free. (In the film version, she runs away from him to her home, seduces him when he finds her, and runs away again the next day.) Joe is caught by his sergeant, and the children who were hiding in the bushes reveal that he has released Carmen and promised to meet her that evening. Joe is then sent to the guardhouse.

Three weeks later, Carmen encounters the boxer, Husky Miller, who decides that he wants her. She is still interested in Joe, and does not disguise her dislike for Husky. Still, Husky demands that his manager have Carmen waiting on the train platform in Chicago in the morning, or the manager will be fired. Rum, Husky's manager, gets to Carmen through two of her girlfriends, Myrt and Frankie. Joe, who is supposed to be released from jail and had planned to meet her there, has not yet arrived. When he does arrive, finally, he reveals that he has only a short leave. Carmen wanted him to go to Chicago with her, but he can't; he has to return to the army base. Before the evening is over, he argues with his superior officer, Sergeant Brown; in a fit of anger, Joe punches him. With Joe already in trouble, this infraction would be the end of his army career. Carmen's plans to go to Chicago become a fortuitous escape route. He escapes one prison for another.

Joe and Carmen take off for Chicago. He has deserted, in addition to assaulting a superior officer, and is on the run in Chicago. By Act 2, Carmen has started seeing Husky on the side. Joe finds out, and is upset; soon after, Carmen has her cards read and finds out that death is pursuing her. Eventually Cindy Lou finds Joe and tells him that his mother is ill. Unfortunately, Joe is so bewitched by Carmen that he is reluctant to leave her for fear of losing her. He finally chooses to go back to see his mother, but plans to return. Joe realizes his duty to his mother; his relationship with Carmen has already destroyed his army career, and threatens to keep him from his other duties. Joe's choice is his first step away from the immoral Carmen, but it comes too late.

With Joe gone, Carmen has again been keeping company with Husky. At Husky's big fight, Joe and Carmen meet again; Joe has gone to the arena to find Carmen. She tells Joe that she is in love with Husky, but Joe will not release her. They fight, and Joe stabs and kills Carmen. Carmen is gone, and Joe is an army deserter and murderer; there is not much left of his life, either. Carmen's insatiable sexual drive has destroyed her life, and his life as well. Joe should have married Cindy Lou and had a nice family; he should have followed his orders and served his country as was his duty. Instead, he was seduced by the sexual black woman, who, as she must, undermined the American institutions of military and family. Joe moved into his "natural" state; Carmen, the sexually aggressive woman, was already in hers. Safety resides in the innocence and virginity of Cindy Lou, but Joe rejects it.

93

There was also a filmed version of *Carmen Jones* (1954). The selling point of the movie was its stars; Dorothy Dandridge played Carmen, Harry Belafonte played Joe, and Ethel Waters was featured in the role of one of Carmen's friends. The film version added another aspect to the tragedy; Dorothy Dandridge was famed in real life as a "mulatta" who frequently portrayed bad tragic mulattas, although she was not as light skinned as some other "real mulatta" actors, like Fredi Washington. Beyond the already tragic circumstances of the jezebel, Dandridge carries the "ghosts" of her other performances of tragic mulattas and her own tragic life with her into this role. Carmen's sexuality and sensuality contrast with the "good girl," Cindy Lou. Whereas Carmen thinks only of herself, Cindy Lou is the self-sacrificing, virtuous woman. Cindy Lou keeps trying to rescue Joe from his lust for Carmen, but she is unsuccessful. She cannot offer what Carmen does; instead, she represents the black woman whose values mimic those of middle-class white America.

Dandridge is not alone in her portrayal of the tragic mulatta/ tragic jezebel. In the 1959 version of *Imitation of Life*, the tragic mulatta finds her escape from blackness in sexuality. As she grows, Sarah Jane also displays her race through the same sexuality that she identifies with freedom. She is a perfect foil for her mother, the mammy, who never is shown as a sexual being. Sarah Jane wants to be white because it offers her privilege. Unfortunately, the only "privilege" available to her is that of sexual license.

Bad girl Sarah Jane runs away from home twice, and finds her new identity in the life of an exotic dancer. Of all possible career choices that could have been hers while she was passing for white, she chooses to express herself by becoming a sexual object, or at least she does in the 1959 version of the film. In the 1934 version, Peola's first job is in a drugstore. By 1959, Annie has lost the ability to save the family through her own ingenuity, and Sarah Jane's employment opportunities have changed. The first time Sarah Jane runs away from home, the impetus is an assault by her white boyfriend. She has an argument with her mother about dating and her

94

racial self-identity, and leaves home. When her mother finds her, she is dancing in a topless club, seemingly popular with the clientele. She is forced to leave when it is discovered that she is not white.

Angry with her mother for having revealed her secret, Sarah Jane reluctantly returns to her home. It is not long before she leaves again, however, this time for Las Vegas, where she lives in a motel. From her dress and that of her roommate, we can assume that she has continued as an exotic dancer or has become a prostitute.

Despite her "success" in the white world, Sarah Jane is still confined to the "lower" regions of it. Her role as dancer/prostitute connects to the mythical unrestricted sexuality of black women's biology and the deviant sexuality of the prostitute; by choosing this role, Sarah Jane embodies the primal, animalistic nature that is supposed to be the realm of the black woman. The exoticized woman's place is on stage; there, she can be viewed by those who might wish to purchase her. Sarah Jane is placed in the position of the object of the white male gaze, and in the old image of jezebel in the hell of carnality. What she sees as her privilege does not make her the subject, and does not really allow her any power.

When examined together, Sarah Jane and Annie provide an interesting comment on the sexual options of black women. They are the only two black women in the film whose characters are developed, and they embody the virgin/whore dichotomy. Annie is the nonsexual mammy, who behaves as any "good" woman should. Sarah Jane, as the mulatta, is tragic and sexual, and even her trespassing into the white world does not broaden her options. The way that mother and daughter must conform to their roles is very different from the way that Lora and her daughter, Susie, do; neither Lora nor her daughter is absolutely a whore, and their sexuality or the lack of it is rationally chosen, not imposed by nature. Even when Lora entertains the option of the casting couch for the sake of her family, she is redeemed from it by falling in love with Steve. Her daughter's schoolgirl crush on him is mitigated by his maturity and his love for Lora. Annie cannot be sexual at all; Sarah Jane is sexual excess and cannot be redeemed.

Because of her innate sexual aggressiveness, the jezebel is always available. She lent herself not only to adaptation in *Carmen Jones*, but also to the play *Anna Lucasta* (1945). A mediocre imitation of Eugene O'Neill's *Anna Christie* (1922), the play was written originally for a Polish immigrant family. The playwright, Philip Yordan, was convinced to change the families involved to blacks in hopes of increasing the possibility of its success. Eartha Kitt played Anna in the 1959 film version.

In this play, there is no doubt that Anna is a prostitute. She has been forced into this life by her father, Joe; when he found her having sex with a young man, he threw her out of the house. With nowhere else to go, she moved to New York and became a "loose woman." She managed to resist the pressure from Eddie, a pimp, to work at his bordello, The Chambers. She might be interested in a sailor, Danny, who is in port at the moment. She can also be a sympathetic character. Resisting the offer of employment in the brothel makes Anna redeemable and capable of love.

Anna's family decides to redeem her. Her father's friend Otis sends his son, Rudolf, to them to marry a nice girl. Anna's brothers soon learn that he is quite rich, and decide that they should figure out a way to bring that money into their family. The only available woman is Anna, and they decide that this country boy will never know the difference. It isn't long before Anna finds out why her family wants her back. She meets Rudolf, and much to everyone's surprise (especially Anna's), they get along well. Their plans for marriage continue, despite Joe's opposition. He does not think that his daughter is the right kind of girl for Rudolf, and he proceeds to try to stop the wedding. Danny arrives, intending to take Anna back to New York and finds that Anna has already married, but Joe has ruined everything. Danny persuades Anna to leave with him, and they return to New York. Anna returns to her old life, including keeping company with Danny and his friend, drinking, dancing, and behaving as her father expected. Rudolf has not forgotten her, however, and goes to New York in search of her eight days later. The two are reunited after the bartender in New York helps them find each other again, and convinces Anna that she should give up her life and become a respectable woman.

In the 1944 production, Anna was played by Hilda Simms, who is very light skinned. As the tragic mulatta prostitute with a heart of gold, Anna is capable of falling in love, and can even be persuaded to leave her other life behind her. Anna chooses love and respectability; by remaining within her community and renouncing her immoral past, she averts her tragic end. In fact, the play is not nearly as proscriptive about black women's roles as some of the other representations of blacks, until one considers what else was presented on Broadway at the same time: *Carmen Jones* opened eight months before *Anna Lucasta*, and both followed productions of *Porgy* and *Porgy and Bess*. As far as mainstream representations of blacks are concerned, *Anna Lucasta*'s coming on the heels of *Carmen Jones* certainly focuses the theatrical audience on mythical representations of "steamy" black life. The critical acclaim for both productions contributed to the iconization of black women's sexuality, for they were popular and had significant runs. Both were later filmed, widening their viewership.

The 1960s and 1970s gave theatre and film audiences other images. In the theatre, the revolution in black-generated art brought plays like *To Be Young, Gifted, and Black*, *The Wedding Band*, and *for colored girls who have considered suicide/when the rainbow is enuf* to mainstream stages. The blaxploitation films of the early 1970s gave us women like Cleopatra Jones, who, while sexy, was a warrior for her people. Rather than chasing men, Jones spent her time hunting down drug lords. Television treated audiences to *Good Times*, which, while still about a family in the ghetto, was saved from falling heavily into cliché when Esther Rolle insisted that she would not play a welfare mother, and that the family had to have a father. *Good Times*, *The Jeffersons*, and other television dramas about blacks continued to offer stereotypes, but the

97

sexual aggressiveness of black women was toned down. However, the jezebel was not forgotten, and reappeared in the 1980s.

Even more astonishing than her return was the locus in which she reemerged: black popular culture. While the black male leaders of the 1960s were infamous for their sexism, they could not match the misogyny of the next generation. Black men's attitudes were fueled by the general conservatism of the 1980s. This period was marked by a small increase in the black middle class; a few black men were better off while the majority were worse off than they had been in the 1970s. Hope in the promise of equality had faded. Some of those who had "made it" turned their backs on their poor relatives and former neighbors, opting for buppiedom and Wall Street. Those who didn't make it were mired in the increasing poverty and crime of the inner cities, and told to "pull themselves up by their own bootstraps" by the Reagan administration and by some blacks. Black men in inner cities were no longer able to vent their rage against "the Man," because in all likelihood, "the Man" was a Brother. They were told that they "should" be able to "make it," because others had done it. Out of this climate grew increasingly macho and misogynistic music, which expressed rage, frequently directed not only at the "cops" but also at the "hoes"— women.

The theatre, unlike film and television, seems largely immune to the reemergence of the jezebel icon; this is partially due to contemporary theatre's liberal audience, and partially due to black theatrical traditions, which will be discussed below. Unfortunately, because of the overall decrease in audiences in the late 1980s and early 1990s, the theatre's impact on the larger American culture has declined. Instead, popular culture transmits images of the new jezebel through film and television.

From MTV to *In Living Color*, the predominant image of black women is that of the sexy whore. Black women have been reassociated with unrestrained sexuality, especially a destructive sexuality. The character is determined not only by action but also by attire. On Madonna, the bustier, garter belt, and other "sex" clothes

looked risqué; on black women, they conjure up images of the jezebel. Madonna may be seen by some as a whore, but others see her
as liberating because she feels free to express her sexuality. Then
again, Madonna is not an icon for white women; black women attempting to express their sexuality by donning this particular costume become an icon for black female sexuality *and* embody the
streetwalker in one step. The "Fly Girl," a regular feature of *In
Living Color* and music videos, becomes the jezebel icon incarnate.
There is no individuality or personality, for she is simply a body to
be exploited. Her body is on display, as those of her ancestors were
displayed for men at slave auctions. Not only is the black woman
of the 1990s expected to conform to this resurrected image, but she
is suspect if she does not; even Salt n' Pepa, a women's rap group,
has adopted the modern jezebel's costume to a degree. A few
women in the rap music scene, like Queen Latifah and the women
of TLC, have managed to avoid the "'ho" image without losing
their audience.

Admittedly, the culture of the music video is limited to
younger audiences, some of whom are able to separate its fiction
from the reality of their own lives. They are much more affected by
the Filmmaker's Talented Tenth of the 1990s: the young black men
who have been adopted by Hollywood. Some recent films have included more varied representations of black women; John Single-
ton's *Higher Learning* has several complex, multidimensional
black female characters, although the smart attractive one must
die in the end. Other films, focusing on the lives of black men, have
resisted placing realistic representations of black women within
their narratives. Even the "first" film of this new generation of
black filmmakers, Spike Lee's 1986 film *She's Gotta Have It*, does
not manage to present women's reality. While films like *Boyz in the
Hood* and *Poetic Justice* do not purport to be women's stories, Lee's
She's Gotta Have It does.

One of the most disturbing things about Lee's first full-length
film is its documentary quality. Shot in black and white, the fictional film resembles real interviews. Most characters have an op-

portunity to address the audience/camera directly, telling the stories of their relationships with Nola Darling. The film is more the stories of the men involved with Nola than it is her own story. Nola is her own best defender, aside from a brief statement by her father. By the end, none of her three male lovers is still involved with her, which undoubtedly biases them. Nola is also the object of the camera's voyeuristic gaze. The "documentarist" perspective in the shooting of the film already implies a voyeuristic audience looking in on Nola's life and dreams, and especially her sexual relationships with her lovers. Nola only looks at the camera; it never looks from her perspective. Her self-explanations appear aimed at a male audience. She never explains herself to any of the women in the film, not even to Opal, her lesbian pursuer. She also has no women friends or confidants.

Nola's "problem" is that she craves sex, with multiple partners. She has three lovers at the start of the film; the rich playboy Noble, the "nice guy" Jamie Overstreet, and the tough (but little) guy Mars Blackmon, played by Lee himself. She is also being pursued by a lesbian neighbor, but Nola is uninterested in her attentions. The men enjoy being with her, but each of them wants her for himself. Lee, as Mars Blackmon, describes her to the audience in one of his direct addresses as a "freak." Her playboy friend Noble describes her as "a lump of clay" that he shaped. To the men, her habits seem strange; she insists on living alone, and will never accompany them to their homes. When they have sex, it is at her apartment, in her bed. Nola doesn't see anything wrong with her self-determined sexuality, but her lovers and their other girlfriends do; these girlfriends are the only other women in the film aside from Opal. There is, of course, nothing wrong with Noble or Jamie seeing more than one woman, clearly demonstrating the double standard implicit in their perspective.

The incident that changes Nola's mind about the life she has been living is the most disturbing segment of the film. Her relationship with Jamie has been developing, including one of the film's most beautiful moments, where Nola and Jamie watch two dancers he has hired for her birthday present. It presents how he sees their relationship's possibilities, captures the beauty of both male and female bodies, and presents the love between blacks as it is rarely seen in the mainstream media. Later, she calls him, wanting him to come to her; he is with another woman, and is resentful at having to leave her because Nola wants him immediately. He arrives at Nola's apartment, they argue, and he rapes her. This rape is configured by the film as a demonstration of how much he loves her, and Nola decides to give up the other two men for him. Nola is portrayed as deserving and even benefiting from such treatment, a notion supported by her decision to marry her rapist. Perhaps Nola was "asking for it" by frustrating the men and having been in control of her sexual relationships. In any case, it is further evidence of a narrative produced by a man's imagination. The abruptness of the attack has made her see the wrong she has been doing, at least temporarily.

Of all of the film's problems, the central one is that none of the men truly understands Nola, not even the one who created her. In a less chauvinistic treatment, the film might have focused not on Nola's freakishness but on the positive aspects of her life. After all, Nola is a woman in control of her own sexuality, up until the point where she decides to please Jamie, and after she has decided she cannot change herself for him. She treats sex as spiritual; her bedroom is a shrine to sex, her bed surrounded by candles that she lights beforehand and extinguishes afterward. She is independent, enjoying a career as a graphic artist, and is basically happy with her life. Aside from the rape, the choice to have sex or not is on her terms. It is frustrating that what could have been a positive film about a black woman exploring her own sexuality instead shows her as unrestrained and immoral sexually. Lee manages, for most of the film, to avoid presenting Nola in a way that suggests pornography. However, the camera eye follows the objectifying male gaze, focusing on her breasts during the sex scene with Jamie. Lee walks a fine line between recreating jezebel and creating a realistic female character with a positive sexuality.

Lee's film is not the origin of these images of black women and their sexuality, but it is representative of the old attitudes reemerging during the 1980s. Nola Darling is also not the "'ho" of rap culture, but she is its immediate predecessor. Nola is an improvement over Carmen Jones and Bess; she is not, however, the heroine she could be. Far from dissenting from the old racist stereotypes of black women as sexually irresponsible, Lee helps legitimate it and gives it new life. Socially, Nola is not the pregnant teenage welfare mother, but morally, there is a connection; she is not pursuing the nuclear family model, and appears sexually liberated.

Not for Us, Thank You

In contrast to the wanton, immoral, black female slut of the white imagination, black female characters presented by black women playwrights of the early to mid-twentieth century were highly moral, and not particularly sexual. Some of this sentiment was due to the socioeconomic class of many of the women playwrights of the African American community; they were likely to be college educated and middle class, and as a result were more determined to characterize blacks as moral. They were acutely conscious of how the characterization of black women as immoral was damaging to them. Hence, their efforts focused on the creation of characters that reflected views of black life that were not present in the arts of the dominant culture, but that they knew from their own personal experience to be realistic.

In conjunction with its repudiation of the mammy, Angelina Weld Grimke's *Rachel* (1916) stands as an originator in this effort as well. The characters in *Rachel* are carefully constructed to avoid sex and sexual references to either men or women. The Lovings and their neighbors seem to be devoid of sexual desire, and sex is never explicitly mentioned. Relationships are confined to the context of marriage and family. None of the women in the play have children out of wedlock, and there is never even a suggestion of participation in sexual activity. Rachel's "children" are the children of the neighborhood, and the one child who lives with her and for whom she cares is an orphan she has adopted. While much of this play is designed to contest the image of the mammy, it also effectively opposes that of the black woman as sexually irresponsible.

Through Rachel, Grimke projects motherhood as a sacred duty, rather than the result of sexual activity. When Rachel speaks of having children, her language is specifically religious and implies immaculate conception:

> I've thought about it a lot, Ma dear, and once I dreamed, and a voice said to me—oh! it was so real—"Rachel, you are to be a mother to little children." Wasn't that beautiful? Ever since I have known how Mary felt at the "Annunciation." (*almost in a whisper*) *God spoke to me through some one, and I believe.* (Hatch and Shine 1974: 143)

Rachel never does have children of her own, because she is conscious of the social limitations that would face any child she had. Her decision to never have children is linked with marriage. She refuses to marry John Strong, not because she doesn't love him, but because she does not want to have children. Children and marriage are inseparable; curiously, the option of marrying for love does not occur to Rachel.

Rachel's view of the lives of Northern urban blacks contrasts sharply with white representations. Rachel's community is not the run-down Catfish Row of the Heywards' *Porgy.* Instead, it appears much like any other middle- or lower middle-class neighborhood. The gamblers, hustlers, and beggars that typify many white representations of black life are absent from the world of Grimke's play. The only people who are unemployed are those who are refused jobs; no one refuses to work. None of the characters has ever been in jail, and no one takes drugs. The absence of sexuality provides an atmosphere devoid of predators, both male and female.

The focus on the lives of the moral, upstanding Loving family demonstrates the humanity of blacks as that "humanity" is seen by a culture that measures virtue by work, chastity, and religious devotion. The blacks in this play in no way reflect the primitivism and exoticism that were fundamental to the white imagination's conception of blacks, and this was one of Grimke's objectives. Blacks of the 1910s and 1920s believed that such representation best benefited blacks. Through it, white audiences would see a part of black life that might well have been invisible to them before. For blacks, the characters could represent black achievements, and roles to which they could aspire in real life. Despite the frustration that racist practices created for Tom, Rachel, and their community, they were worthy of better treatment. This possibility is open to all blacks, not only those whose "white blood" is evident.

One characteristic that typifies the black intellectual communities of the early twentieth century is the support for black women's struggles to be recognized. Paula Giddings notes that in this period within the black community, there was an impetus for "black women [to] be appreciated not only for their strength but for their feminine attributes as well" (1984: 184). Black men and women were acutely aware of the dominant culture's damaging representations of black women. The black journal *The Messenger*'s editorial goals, according to Giddings, were to show the black woman who was "beautiful, industrious, talented, and successful" (185). What Grimke had shown in her 1916 play, Marita Bonner reiterated and personalized in the 1920s. In the introduction to *Frye Street and Environs*, the collected works of Bonner, editor Joyce Flynn remarks that

> The essay [On Being Young—a Woman—and Colored] explores a dichotomy seen in many works by Afro-American writers: the dichotomy between inner reality and socially sanctioned gender roles. Bonner laments the fact that, like all black women, she is seen primarily as "a gross collection of uncontrolled desires." (1987: xv)

In the article, Bonner asks, "Why do they see a colored woman only as a gross collection of desires, all uncontrolled, reaching out for their Apollos and the Quasimodos with avid discrimination?" (Flynn 1987: 5). The implication is that in their quest for sexual fulfillment, black women would choose any man indiscriminately. This notion is certainly apparent in characters like Bess, who willingly chooses to be first with Crown, and later with Sportin' Life as well as with Porgy. Carmen Jones, too, eventually seeks the attentions of Husky when she becomes bored with Joe.

Although she herself was middle class, Bonner's early work in particular focuses on the lives of the black working class, reflecting her knowledge about the black communities in both Washington, D.C., and Chicago, where she lived for many years. One of her early plays, *The Pot Maker* (1927), is a short piece that condemns the indiscriminate wanton black woman. Calling it "A Play to be Read," Bonner places the action inside the home of Elias and his parents. Elias has been called to preach, much to the dismay of his wife, Lucinda. She is frustrated in her relationship with him primarily because he seems to have no motivation. They have lived with his parents because he does not have a substantial job and cannot afford to move them into their own house. She expresses her dissatisfaction by having an affair with Lew, who is an unlikable character, described among other things as being "overbearing" and "overfat." Elias and his parents (particularly his mother) are aware of Lucinda's unfaithfulness.

Elias creates a parable that he plans to give as a sermon in an upcoming church service. The tale is of a pot maker who has a room full of clay pots. He explains to the pots that he is going to fill each of them, and he expects them to remain upright and to not spill any of their contents, no matter what might happen. Those who remain standing when he returns in the morning will become gold; those who spill only a little will become silver, and those who cannot resist and fall over will be tin. One of the pots tells the pot maker that it has a crack; the pot maker repairs the pot without judging it or asking how it came to be cracked.

105

The pots are left overnight, and after storms and frightening noises, the pot maker returns, awarding each pot its due, according to the standards he set the previous day. The implication is that God is a pot maker, and that salvation is there for the asking; but those who are not obedient and do not resist temptation are only tin.

After Elias's practice sermon, Lew leaves, and Lucinda prepares to go out for the evening. It is evident to both Elias and his mother that Lucinda intends to go meet Lew. Mother prevents Lucinda from wearing her good shoes out of the house, and Elias delays her as long as possible. Elias has set a trap for Lew, and Lew falls into a well as planned. Lucinda goes after him, and likewise falls in while trying to help him. Elias does not want to lose Lucinda, and he also drowns in the well trying to save her.

On the surface, the message doesn't seem much different from that of mainstream representations. Lucinda is immoral in her relationship with Lew, and her lasciviousness leads to the destruction of herself and the men. Bonner makes it clear that the conscience of the community, represented by Mother, does not approve of Lucinda's illicit relationship. She does all that she can to prevent Lucinda's departure. Elias tries to persuade her with Christianity, but she is not willing to listen. Elias, Lucinda, and Lew all have "cracks," in the language of the parable. None of the characters are beautiful or sympathetic. However, they appear not as the norm, but as a problem within the black community. Lucinda and Lew's behavior is clearly immoral rather than amoral; they and the community are aware that what they are doing is wrong. They do not act out of nature or biological compulsion, but out of their own flagrant disdain for the moral codes of the community. Their deaths are the result of their transgression of the moral codes. Elias also violates the community's ethic by refusing to work, and later by setting a deadly trap for Lew. By biblical standards, all three of them have violated fundamental principles of Christian morality. Not only do they act wrongly, but the three are conscious of their violation of community moral standards.

Many of the other plays of the period of the Harlem Renaissance display a similar commitment to conventional morality. While W. E. B. Du Bois condemned the aversion to representing blacks as sexual beings, these women and many of their colleagues, like Georgia Douglas Johnson, Mary Burrill, and Eulalie Spence put forth a conscious effort to persuade both black and white audiences that blacks were not the amoral, animalistic creatures they were believed to be. Whether their representations were of Northern city life or Southern rural life, these playwrights felt it important to focus on the reality they knew. Middle-class women, they had a solid Christian moral base; they were aware that even for poor blacks, Christianity was an important element of life. While the traditions of poor blacks may have been more ecstatic than those of the middle class, Christianity was a common core of life. In focusing on the morals inherent in both communities, the black women playwrights of the early twentieth century hoped to make blacks appear more like whites, particularly as white values were considered "human" values. These playwrights would also continue the projects of the black club women of the nineteenth century, persuading those blacks who did not wish to emulate the images of whites that there were other options.

New Concepts of Sexuality

As the century progressed, black women remained conscious of the representations of them by the dominant culture. Efforts to mitigate the damage caused by the proliferation of the jezebel myth continued, but black women playwrights also became conscious of a need for a positive view of sexuality. Patricia Hill Collins quotes Cheryl Clarke as saying in 1983, "We [black women] have expended much energy trying to debunk the racist mythology which says our sexuality is depraved" (1990: 165). In the late 1960s and early 1970s, feminist consciousness informed the ideas of a new generation of women. There was still a need to combat the mythological jezebel, but unlike their predecessors, these women were also aware that they needed to be able to present a positive sexuality for black women. bell hooks presents the dilemma in the form of a question in her book *Black Looks*:

> How and when will black females assert sexual agency in ways that liberate us from the confines of colonized desire, of racist/sexist imagery and practice? (1992: 75)

During the 1950s and early 1960s, the problem of the stereotyped image was apparent to many. Lorraine Hansberry, in *A Raisin in the Sun* (1959) and *To Be Young, Gifted, and Black* (1970), expresses the concept of a black morality and exposes racist mythologizing. The character Beneatha dates, but refuses physical contact with George Murchison. In Lena Younger's house, the children are expected to follow the rules no matter how old they are. There are not, nor have there been, extramarital affairs in the Younger household. Lena does not want Walter Lee to invest in a liquor store because it violates her values.

Three of the characters in *To Be Young, Gifted, and Black* describe encounters using the same speech:

> the white boys in the street, they look at me and think of sex. They look at me and that's *all* they think. . . . Baby, you could be Jesus in drag—but if you're brown, they're sure you're selling! (Quoted in Collins 1984: 73)

The phenomenon that Hansberry documents in this monologue reflects the effects of the image of black women as sexually available. Robert Staples documents the history of the presentation of black women as not simply sexually available, but as presumed prostitutes, in his work *The Black Woman in America* (1973). His study finds black women to be the most visible prostitutes; "with sufficient accuracy, we can designate the typical Black prostitute as a streetwalker and the white prostitute as a call girl" (82). By plying her trade on the street, the black prostitute becomes in fact the iconic picture of "prostitute." This image then is transferred to any black woman who walks down a street. Biblical Jezebel, the temple prostitute, becomes the contemporary prostitute, complete with black skin. The sexuality that black women embodied for white slave owners and employers becomes that of the available black woman whose body can still be purchased for sexual pleasure.

The icon of the jezebel, through years of representation and acculturation, has become ingrained in the American consciousness. The construction of the virgin/whore dichotomy has implicit in it a white/black dichotomy; it becomes very difficult for black women to express or represent their sexuality because it stands open to misinterpretation. The surge of feminism during the 1970s did provide some space in which black female sexuality could be reconceptualized.

First among theatrical representations is Ntozake Shange's *for colored girls who have considered suicide/when the rainbow is enuf* (1977). While Shange received criticism for the male characters she created, little was said that acknowledged her contribution to the revision of the representation of the sexual black woman. In an interview, Shange stated, "There is a lush quality to women's sexuality that we have ignored because of the stark realities of pornography and the way men treat us as sexual objects. Hopefully, my characters bring out some of the richness and the sensuality that I think is inherent in a female existence" (Betsko and Koenig 1987: 375).

for colored girls . . . delves into the lives, including sexuality, of black women; black women tell their own stories of their experiences with sex. They are subjects with sexuality, rather than objects of male sexuality. The Lady in Yellow describes her first sexual encounter with a high school sweetheart:

> bobby started lookin at me
> yeah
> he started looking at me real strange

like i waz a woman or somethin/
started talkin real soft
in the backseat of that ol buick
WOW
by daybreak
i just cdnt stop grinnin (Shange 1977: 9)

The Lady in Yellow revels in her memories of a positive first experience, one that Shange takes care to reveal not as wanton sexuality
but as the beauty of a shared moment.

Another section of Shange's choreopoem explores the trauma
of rape, particularly when the woman knows her rapist. While the
section focuses particularly on rape by friends or acquaintances, it
reiterates the difficulties that black women have historically had in
prosecuting their rapists. It also contradicts the myth that black
women are always sexually available (and thus essentially un-
rapeable), as they are typically portrayed.

Many criticisms of the play by black men focus on the character of Beau Willie Brown; they claim that the play presents black
men in a bad light. Although Beau Willie is a reprehensible character, there are other representations of black men. The Lady in
Brown describes her discovery of Toussaint L'Ouverture, her "first
blk man," in the adult section of the library (1977: 27):

TOUSSAINT L'OUVERTURE
became my secret lover at the age of 8
i entertained him in my bedroom
widda flashlight under my covers
way inta the night/we discussed strategies
how to remove white girls from my hopscotch games
&etc. (28)

Not only do the women relate their joys and pains of being
involved with men, but Shange also explores the women's relationships with each other. The Lady in Purple speaks of the bonds

110

between three women who do not allow the love relationship of one of them to destroy their emotional connection. When the relationship is over, the one who has been hurt is comforted by the women friends she nearly abandoned:

> she held her head on her lap
> the lap of her sisters soakin up tears
> each understandin how much love stood between them
> how much love between them
> love between them
> love like sisters (44)

The bonds between the women create a network of support; the element of competition around the issues of their individual relationships with men is decreased. From this point until the end of the piece, there is an emphasis on the beauty of black women, and the project of self-making despite the forces of the outside world; of finding god in one's self and loving her fiercely.

Shange is one among many black women playwrights and novelists who, reviving and revising the traditions of the 1920s, sought to accurately present the lives of black women. While they produce a wide variety of lived experience, urban and rural, different classes, contemporary and historic lives, they have in common a refutation of the jezebel icon. Aisha Rahman's 1977 play *Unfinished Women Cry in No Man's Land While a Bird Dies in a Gilded Cage* takes place in part at the Hide-A-Wee Home for Unwed Mothers during the 1950s, yet presents the pregnant young women not as amoral sexual creatures, but real women confronting pregnancy and coming into their own womanhood.

Alexis DeVeaux's *The Tapestry* (1976) presents a young black woman who is coming to terms with her individuality and taking control of her life. In the introduction to the play, Margaret Wilkerson comments that "DeVeaux presents the black woman as a political, social, and sexual being" (1986: 136). While studying for her bar exams, Jet, the young law student, must also struggle with her relationship with her boyfriend, Axis, a jazz musician, and her friendship with Lavender, the beautiful radio disk jockey who lives upstairs. *The Tapestry* is DeVeaux's vehicle to present "the black woman in relation to her eros, her sexuality" (Tate 1983: 55).

One of the problems that Jet must resolve is that of her relationship with Axis. Axis has said:

> ill be glad when this is all over baby
> dont get me wrong
> you know im a funny man
> i dont like sharing my woman with no law school
> textbooks   *all the time* (149)

It soon becomes obvious that Axis is interested in Lavender, and while they hide their relationship for some time, Axis eventually attempts to use his relationship with Lavender to pressure Jet into abandoning her legal career.

Unlike her predecessors in the early part of the century, DeVeaux is not afraid to show sensuality between black men and women on stage. In the first scene, she has Jet and Axis kissing and touching each other, which is presented as more sensual than sexual. In the following scene, Jet and Axis have a scene that shows their growing conflict, but also their emotional and physical connection. With the lights dimmed on stage and music playing, Jet and Axis make love on the couch-bed; it is still devoid of any air of the sordid.

It becomes obvious in the next scene that Lavender and Jet have very different goals and expectations. Lavender is surprised to hear that Jet does not feel secure even though she "got a man/ of [her] own" (169). Jet explains herself:

> i want to be defined in my own terms
> not somebody elses
> i want to leave my mark on the world
> make it all worth something

something more than working my way
into old age and a social security check
i see things to be done
so many things (170)

Lavender doesn't understand, and to her the most important thing is having a man and, more specifically, pleasing him. Ultimately, this is Axis's idea of a woman's role. Near the beginning of Act 2, Axis and Jet argue over her "womanhood," the implication being that Jet's behavior is not womanly because of her dedication to something other than Axis. She is angry about Axis's impropriety, and in her subsequent conversation with Lavender, the relationship between Axis and Lavender is revealed. At the end of the play, Jet leaves to take her exam, having been abandoned by both Lavender and Axis. However, Jet's choices seem to be responsible ones, ones for which she can be admired.

Jet's goals are to do what she can and to make what changes in the world that she can; to do that, she has to separate herself from the expectations that both Axis and Lavender have about women's roles. She cannot be the jezebel and accomplish anything, and she has redefined her role as a woman. Axis and Lavender's ideas about what a woman should be are profoundly different, and they consequently resist Jet's attempts to redefine her own role, in which she is neither a mother/nurturer nor a sexual object.

A more recent contribution is Cheryl West's *Jar the Floor* (1989). West presents four generations of women, revealing the complex relationships between mothers and daughters, while including some serious and taboo subjects. Vennie, the youngest of the women, is a lesbian, and brings her white lover home (the lover has breast cancer and has already had one breast removed). Her mother, Maydee, is a university professor anxiously awaiting her tenure decision. Maydee has eschewed most relationships with men, in direct contrast with her mother, Lola, who has had a long string of lovers. We later discover that Maydee was raped by one of

Lola's lovers. West reveals a variety of black women's sexualities without resorting to stereotypes or invoking the jezebel icon, while also departing from both black and white classic representations of motherhood.

While African American women have found a theatrical outlet to express their new visions of themselves and their sexuality and revisions of the lives of black women throughout history, they have had difficulty translating those images onto film. Although Hansberry's *A Raisin in the Sun* was made into a successful Hollywood film, we have already seen that the film was a departure from Hansberry's original. Mainstream cinema has not had many black female characters who did not fall into one or another of the stereotypes or icons of black femaleness. This void begged to be filled; unfortunately, there have been few films that could fill it. If audience support can be a measure of the desire for new images of black women, then Julie Dash's 1991 film *Daughters of the Dust*, which was shown to full houses, has begun a trend toward filling that void.

Dash was not able to get mainstream distribution for her film, but its Sundance award encouraged Kino International to release it, and it was presented in art film houses all over the country. There was not much publicity for the film; yet, when I first went to see it in Washington, D.C., both of the showings at the Biograph repertory theatre were sold out. The line stretched for two blocks. It was shown later for a longer engagement at another small cinema, where it again had sizable audiences. *Daughters of the Dust* has been hailed as the first African American woman's film, and Dash's characters were consciously created to challenge the icons of the dominant culture, including the mammy, as we saw earlier, and the jezebel.

The sexuality of the women and men of Ibo Landing is never presented in a way that would imply animalistic or amoral sexuality. The fact that the film takes place in 1902 may have some influence on that, but it is not the whole reason. The representation of sexuality is much more sensuality; it is also not exclusively heterosexual. Amazingly, the film is able to treat the relationship between two women without the baseness that was evident in Steven Spielberg's treatment of Alice Walker's *The Color Purple* (1985).

Dash takes advantage of her multigenerational film to represent several different types of sexual relationships. There are the characters Newlywed Man and Newlywed Woman, who have two scenes where they are seen alone together. In the first, there is an implication of their having sex; Dash films the scene without ever presenting their sexual relations in any pornographic sense. Their actions are understood, without any of the visual overtness that has become abundant in contemporary film. They are undressing, but are never actually seen in the nude. In a later scene, the two of them are alone on the beach, one leaning against a tree. One of the sentiments that characterizes their scenes together is playfulness; there is also a palpable sense of the beauty of their relationship. Neither of them embodies the mythic aggressiveness ascribed to blacks; their romance is gentle, caring, and loving and lacks any sense of amorality.

There is also the blossoming love of Iona, one of the Peazant teenagers, and St. Julian Last Child, the last Cherokee in the Sea Islands. The two ride off together near the end of the film. They have planned her "rescue," and St. Julian arrives at the slip just before the boat leaves to carry the family north. We learn of St. Julian's feelings for Iona in a letter that he leaves for her, and that she reads to her sisters and cousins:

> Iona, with the greatest respect for yourself, and the Peazant family, I beg that you stay by my side here on this island. . . . We are the young, the eager up from slavery. . . . Eager to learn a trade, eager to make a better life for ourselves and our children who will follow. Our love is a very precious, very fragile flowering of our most innocent childhood association. . . . Iona, as I walk towards the future, with your heart embracing mine, everything seems new, everything seems good, everything seems possible. (Dash 1992: 88–91)

115

Their love is presented as idyllic and innocent, culminating in the heroic "rescue" of Iona. Iona is in the boat with the members of the family who are leaving to go north, obviously nervous, hoping that St. Julian will arrive in time. He rides up on his horse, and Iona runs from the boat, while her mother, Haagar, tries to run after her. St. Julian lifts Iona up onto the horse, and they ride off together. That is the only time the two of them are seen together, making complete the image of romantic love they represent.

The third "couple" to challenge mainstream representations is that of Yellow Mary and Trula. Dash courageously tackles the challenge of creating black female characters who are not heterosexual (Dash says that Yellow Mary, at least, is bisexual) and who also have been, by implication, prostitutes. Mary and Trula are usually seen together, and their relationship is only implied; it is never physically represented or stated on film. There is a gentleness and tenderness between them, and a constant sense that they are aware of something hidden from the others on the island. There is no romanticization about their involvement in prostitution, either; Mary explains to her cousin Eula that when she was sent away to work as a maid or nanny for a white family, she was raped by her employer. This left her few options, because she had already been violated. She is not absolutely proud of her profession, but she is adamant that it was not something she chose.

Sexual and Racial Domination

The icon of the jezebel, as we have seen, has presented black women as unrestrained sexual animals. In part, this representation of black women has maintained misconceptions of biology and genetics that justified racism and slavery. Although it is no longer generally accepted that blacks are biologically inferior to whites, there is still a tendency to conceptualize them as sexually uncontrolled by nature. As Ann Du Cille comments in her article "Blue Notes on Black Sexuality,"

Black is taken to mean sensational, licentious, raunchy. It is, I would argue, an internally dysfunctional reading of the racial subject and the semiotics of the black body that categorize moral value by color and by class and defines "authentic black-ness" as the absence thereof. (1993: 422)

This has been the case particularly with black women, who were made to bear the responsibility for black men's alleged aggressive sexuality as well as that of the allegedly helpless white men who were "forced" to rape them. As Du Cille also notes, Sigmund Freud popularized the connection of female sexuality to Africa, in which the black female, whose ancestral origins are Africa, functioned as an icon in the racial and sexual ideology of the West.

The construction of the black female as a sexual creature also denied her the quality of femininity, at least in the eyes of an American society that viewed the mythic virginal, sexless white woman as the paragon of the feminine. Although she was not feminine, she was the ultimate sex object. This was particularly the case if she were light skinned; the mulatta presented a woman who, because of her whiteness, was attractive and yet, because of her blackness, was allegedly sexual. The icon became more noticeable during the mid-twentieth century, when the quintessential bad sexual woman was presented as the mulatta, particularly in the characters of Carmen Jones and Sarah Jane of *Imitation of Life*.

That black women were often represented in film, literature, and other visual arts as prostitutes reveals the position of black women even more blatantly. As Collins states, "prostitution represents the fusion of exploitation for an economic purpose—namely, the commodification of Black women's sexuality—with the demeaning treatment afforded to pets" (1990: 175). Of course, the black prostitute does not only function as an icon of the black woman. She also exists in reality at the bottom of the sex-for-hire world, accentuating her economic situation.

Even the contemporary representation of the black woman in mainstream film has not come as far as it should. The 1996 film

117

Waiting to Exhale was praised by many critics, whereas others, like bell hooks, took a much closer look at the images in it. While the women characters were decidedly middle and upper middle class, their only concerns were material and social. Money and men were their primary objectives, particularly for the conventionally more attractive (thin with hair weaves or otherwise straightened hair). Their pursuit of men as the crucial ingredient for happiness placed them more often than not on their backs—once again representing commodified black female sexuality. The women's community work, which was included in the book, disappeared entirely from the film.

The jezebel as an icon was, originally, a creation of the white imagination, which contributed to the justification of the the subjugation of both black women and men. This image, along with other demeaning images of black women, was consciously opposed by blacks. In the early part of the twentieth century, African American women playwrights attempted to change the jezebel image by presenting black women not as sexual wantons, but as moral, upstanding citizens who were essentially asexual. They hoped that by presenting an alternative to the jezebel icon, blacks would be treated as humans instead of as children or animals. Later artists were able to see that the constrictions Christian morality placed on black women denied them the possibility of a positive sexuality. By the end of the twentieth century, the presentation of positive black female sexuality as an alternative to the destructive animalistic sexual woman is still a necessary project. The scope of the project has broadened somewhat, as many contemporary images that characterize black women as jezebels come from the black community as well as from the dominant culture.

Chapter 4

Representation and Resistance in an Antiblack World

I think that the eighties have reinstated a stereotyped image of blacks.

—Charles Gordone

If, as Alice Walker says, "Resistance is the secret of joy," then African American women playwrights and film directors have repeatedly voiced their joy throughout the twentieth century (1992: 281). As we have seen, resistance to the racist stereotypes of the white imagination has formed the core of black women's theatrical expression. While there is often resistance in feminist theatre theory to realistic theatre (see Dolan 1991, Case 1988, and Austin 1990), many African American women have used, and continue to use, realism to challenge the icons of mainstream theatre and film. By using realism as a base, these women create images meant to respond directly to those in the mainstream media. Responding to what is depicted as realism, these women formulate images that more accurately depict blacks, particularly black women. These artists pave the way for the development of the black woman warrior, the quintessential image of visual resistance. We have already seen her in resistance to all three icons, particularly in plays and films written and produced between 1960 and 1990.

From the very beginnings of dramatic literature written by black women, the concept that was first named "womanist" by

Alice Walker has been evident as the driving force behind this image of the warrior. This image, unlike those of the mammy, mulatto, or jezebel, is not monolithic. From Angelina Weld Grimke to Georgia Douglas Johnson to Lorraine Hansberry to Julie Dash, the black woman artist has endeavored to portray the variety of experience of black women in America. The warrior woman became a conscious image later; the melding of the civil rights and feminist movements encouraged the development of black women who were "race warriors" in an expanded sense. They begin with characters like Lena, Ruth, and Beneatha in *A Raisin in the Sun* (1959), but grow and develop. In film, some of the women in the "blaxploitation" genre are representations of those warriors; the character Cleopatra Jones is an excellent example. The film *Cleopatra Jones* (1973) manages to depict a strong black woman without resorting to any of the three icons (unlike many of the films starring Pam Grier, which rely heavily on gratuitous female nudity). Cleopatra is in control of her life; she fights to save her community from drug pushers and corrupt police officers.

The women in Ntozake Shange's *for colored girls . . .* (1977) are more strongly influenced by traditional feminism, although Shange's inclusion of positive images of black men along with the very negative Beau Willie Brown gives it some balance. The "womanist" vision illustrated is a legacy of the history of remarkable black women. The warrior images celebrated the strength, beauty, and wisdom of black women.

For all the efforts of the numerous African American women playwrights and filmmakers, the icons of the antiblack imagination have not yet been banished from the stage or screen. While the mammy-mulatto-jezebel trio is more likely to appear on the screen than on the stage, "masterpieces" like *Show Boat* and *Porgy and Bess* are revived from time to time, keeping the images alive. Occasionally, they are directed in such a way that the original stories are viewed from a critical historical standpoint, thereby mitigating the apparent innocence of the images; more often, they are presented with little or no consideration for their role in perpetuating racist iconography. The images are still being presented to contemporary audiences who are already familiar with the icons.

By now we are well aware that the trio of icons of the black woman has remained a part of American culture. They have remained despite years of attempts to correct or eradicate them. Racism in the United States has not been eliminated, and the icons have only been somewhat modified. This is not to say that there is a strict cause and effect relationship between racism and racist stereotypes, but the two are intertwined in the cultural production that supports the status quo. The racist icons have remained because racism remains, and vice versa.

What is accomplished by the mythologizing of black women? Myth does not function outside of culture; it has profound resonances within that culture. Myth has the power to affect the whole spectrum of social and economic relationships. These icons, which function as myths, have created ideas about black women that serve to maintain systemic antiblack racism. According to the myths, black women are infantile, and are therefore unqualified for positions of power. We see this boldly in contemporary antiaffirmative action rhetoric. The notion persists that blacks who are hired under affirmative action laws are unqualified, and would be unable to achieve by their own merit. For some, the abolishment of affirmative action laws intimates that equality between blacks and whites has been reached. There is an assumption of a "level playing field," the idea that all citizens, regardless of race or gender, have equal access and opportunity. Recent reports from organizations like the NAACP and the National Urban league do not support this notion. The sentiment that underlies most of the rhetoric is that blacks are unqualified.

Blacks' alleged immaturity is underlined by their alleged inability to use language properly. Black women are inherently sexual beings, if we believe the mythology; a woman who always wants sex can hardly be raped. The mulatta wants to be white, and will

121

attempt to pass if she is light enough, or so says the myth of the tragic mulatta.

These images, placed before an audience, do not simply entertain. When the stereotypes are carried within the collective consciousness of a society (i.e., when they become icons), they engender illusions, expectations, and limitations. African American cultural critics and artists have recognized this and have challenged the icons that, despite their efforts at eliminating them, still exist. The creation of alternatives to the icons is not merely an aesthetic exercise, but part of greater cultural and political resistance to anti-black racism.

The connections between the racism in the projects and in the policies of the United States have, until very recently, been opaque. The actively liberal population has concerned itself with remedying the great wrongs and injustices done to blacks while desiring to maintain its own place of privilege. Like many middle-class blacks, they believe that racism is the territory only of working-class or conservative whites. Not only do they perceive racism as not their problem, but they believe that it does not directly affect them. However, as Gloria Joseph comments in *Common Differences*,

> The problem of racism was supposedly solved in the Sixties; therefore, Blacks who don't make it have no one to blame but themselves. This, of course, is not true. The record from the Seventies clearly shows that conditions for Blacks have worsened. [The economic gap between black and white families increased in both absolute and relative terms.] (1981: 180)

Many white "liberals" have appropriated the cause of racism, carefully supporting those images that they deem "realistic," especially those of poor inner-city blacks, and condemning those that are not, especially those of middle-class blacks. As a result, blackness is viewed as a monolith; somewhere, it is believed, there is a "true" black experience that must be recognized.

While white liberal intentions are good, the universalizing of

122

black experience must be seen as a continuation of earlier efforts to maintain stereotypes rather than to dispel them. *The Cosby Show* was much maligned by white liberals (and some blacks) for showing an unrealistic view of black families; however, it is only unrealistic if you believe or maintain that true black culture must be confined to the inner-city ghettoes. There are black families with two professional parents, large houses, and swimming pools and tennis courts in their backyards. The assertion that *The Cosby Show* had "sold out" and merely imitated "white values" assumed that white culture was the model, and *Cosby* was an imitation, denying the validity or existence of a middle-class black culture that is different from that of either poor inner-city black experience or white middle-class experience. Is it yet another racist stereotype to believe that blacks cannot gain a measure of "success" as defined by American culture—money, property, education? The liberal criticism of *The Cosby Show* is not an isolated incident. In an interview with Chris Gilmer, Ruby Dee commented on criticisms of her portrayal of Amanda in Tennessee Williams's *The Glass Menagerie*:

> We are just not accustomed to thinking of the universal applications outside of a certain group, because the stereotypes are so in place. That really seemed to be a question in some minds, that the men were not cooks or waiters or in one of those jobs to which Black people were confined so long. (Gilmer 1992: 243)

Some of the audience members of the Arena Stage production thought it was unrealistic that there could be black "gentleman callers" and people who worked in jobs not traditionally held by blacks.

Race, the perceptions of race, and the politics of race are fundamental to American culture. This has become particularly evident today, as Congress attempts to remove affirmative action and civil rights programs that were created in the 1960s. For all that we thought had been accomplished in the 1960s and 1970s, the

123

1980s and 1990s have proved that racism cannot be legislated away. Typically, the expressions of racism in the culture and in politics have been less blatant; this is no longer the case. The current attacks on the welfare system and affirmative action are aimed at white fears of a black population stepping out of its prescribed arena. Blacks who are successful are assumed to be underqualified; a black who manages to find a job in a tight job market "got the job because he or she is black."

Americans still typically see racial problems as an issue of black versus white. The country has fully invested itself in this ancient duality, effectively erasing other nonwhites in the culture. In some measure, then, both politics and culture are implicated in the maintenance of both the duality and the positions of "self," i.e., human, and nonhuman, bestial, i.e., the black that it creates. As Lewis Gordon explains in *Bad Faith and Antiblack Racism*,

> [D]uality is a projection onto the human species which calls for human beings to be what they are not. This masked effort also requires the motivation of a passion or interest in preserving the duality. . . . The point at which the value "superior" is attributed to one and the value of "inferior" to another is the point at which each group becomes a deep or ontological denial of human reality. (1995a: 97–98)

The dominant cultural production, whether film, theatre, or television, tends to support the maintenance of this duality that has, in effect, become an essential part of American culture and identity, or American ontology. In Jacquie Jones's words, "racism is institutionalized, i.e., well organized, and its assumptions are woven into every aspect of our most intimate transactions" (1994: 12). It is at this point that it becomes evident that "art" and "politics" are not separate entities.

The idea that all art is inherently political has been a given throughout this study. Any act of representation supports a particular view of groups of individuals. This was certainly the belief of such playwrights as Angelina Weld Grimke, and of leaders like W. E. B. Du Bois. In addition, it must be taken into account that for many people in the United States, their only experience of people of other races comes from the cultural representations of them. It is even more important, then, that representation is recognized as an agent that affects the social and political consciousness of the population. The semiotics of these icons as cultural representation is inherent in Umberto Eco's definition:

> Signs stand for something else in some respect or capacity. "In some respect" means that they are not a mere duplicate of the thing they stand for; "in some capacity" means that signs represent something else because of some correlated features that must be thoroughly described. (Quoted in Mast and Cohen 1985: 196)

In short, then, the signs, or icons, of the black woman that have become part of popular culture come to represent all black women; they are not duplicates of black women, but they do stand for them in the culture.

Contemporary Trends, Contemporary Theatre

Where does all of this leave us? In the present climate, we have to wonder if perhaps all past efforts of black and white artists to eradicate racism through theatrical production have been fruitless, and if we as artists should refocus our efforts. The April 1995 issue of *American Theatre* cites trends in American theatre: the nation's regional theatres are relying more on subscriber and ticket sales than ever (particularly as government funding has eroded), and the audience for live theatre has decreased steadily in the past five years. Who goes to the theatre anymore? Who are we trying to reach with our visions of ourselves and our country?

One of the noticeable trends in the contemporary regional the-

125

atre is the inclusion of the 1990s buzzword, *multiculturalism*. The practice of this term varies from region to region, and from theatre to theatre. In some places, it means a serious commitment to casting practices and play selection. The Seattle Group Theatre is a fine example of this type of theatre; the Group is committed to producing plays that include the variety of American experience. Recent productions have included plays on Chicano and African American experience, as well as projects like Ping Chong's *Undesirable Elements* (1995), a piece created to explore differences among Seattle's ethnic communities. Their commitment to multiculturalism extends from their administrative staff to their production teams, encouraging cooperation and acceptance of difference. In other theatres, multicultural means that the theatre might present a play by a black playwright during February—Black History Month. While the latter practice is rife with tokenism, there still remains the possibility of reaching a predominantly white audience that may be better able to understand of the situation of blacks, present or historical. The former theatre type usually signals a more liberal audience base; for a theatre that actively embraces American ethnic cultures to survive, it has to appeal to a large enough population to support it.

To some extent, I wonder if any live theatrical performance can move any audience member to confront her or his own racism. In the liberal theatre, when we are not preaching to the converted, we are attempting to communicate with those who readily admit that racism still exists but who feel that it is not within their power to change anything. During many an audience post-play discussion, I have heard liberal white people remark that "I don't see color" or "I don't understand why that character was so angry." From a less informed, more culturally isolated audience, such comments would be expected, but this type of response from a liberal, urban white population is disheartening.

First, to deny "seeing color" is to deny difference. The erasure of difference has never been the goal of multiculturalism or of ethnic artists; rather, we as black theatre artists, playwrights, directors, and scholars have sought to present the multiplicity of our culture. The wish is not to "become white" or to erase our physical and cultural differences. Instead, we have hoped that we would be recognized as something other and more than the universalized icons that the dominant white culture has imposed upon us.

Second, while some of our self-representations will be of the type that present our positive, happy, "normal" existence, we cannot deny the anger that exists because of the continued discrimination and racism we experience on a daily basis. Many in the liberal middle-class white audience are afraid of the presentation of black rage. Whether they persist in their belief that racism has been obliterated, or whether they are offended at the implication of their own complicity with racist structures, they feel that the representation of the pain of being black in American society is not a legitimate subject for dramatic literature. If it is important to show how far we have come, it is equally important to show where we have been, and how far we have yet to go. Unfortunately, many of those in the audience will refuse to see the less beautiful side of black American life.

In fact, there is a palpable sense that the representation of the lives of blacks on stage is threatening to some audiences. This trepidation expresses itself in many ways, from theatre organizations that shy away from more controversial plays to those that choose not to include voices from segments of society other than white and middle class. Ntozake Shange comments that

> White people get scared of black people who dream because our dreams are allegedly about taking something from somebody. They might be if we were fully in power and we owned everything we didn't have a right to. (Quoted in Lester 1990: 55)

This idea, while it has been subtle in past years, is among the ideas that are fueling the current backlash against civil rights. The arguments in Congress to eliminate affirmative action cloak the idea that blacks (and women and other minorities, to a lesser extent) are taking jobs and contracts away from whites. Implicit in this thinking is that white males by nature deserve certain jobs, and that underqualified blacks are stealing these white privileges. This sensibility echoes the white fear of the mulatta who passes for white, who is viewed as taking advantage of privileges not rightfully hers.

Not surprisingly, black theatre artists and scholars continue to struggle to have our voices heard. Until very recently, talk of the backlash against feminism has largely overshadowed the conservative backlash against inclusion of all other perspectives, and the legitimacy of the study of "minority" cultures. In the theatre, this has led to decreased funding for the arts; while the largest outcry was over "obscenity," the cuts in arts funding have affected small ethnic theatres and artists as well as gay and lesbian theatres and artists. The difficulties are often increased for small ethnic theatres, because their audiences are not always able to support the theatres financially from ticket sales alone.

Multiculturalism is a current byword in most universities and departments. Yet, as in the liberal white theatre audience, there is little examination of practices, and little actual inclusion. While one of the most important tenets of multiculturalism is inclusion, more often than not ethnic-based studies are presented in "special" classes and departments. For example, rather than including the history of Asian, Chicano, Latino, Native, and African Americans in a general course on American theatre, those perspectives are often "saved" for a special seminar. It is as though these perspectives and literatures are not truly a part of "American" culture; they are relegated to the status of subculture.

Clearly, the efforts of generations of people, black and white, to remove societal racism and race privilege have not yet been successful. This leaves us with an unfortunate dilemma: do we continue to work against racism, particularly in the theatre, or do we abandon hope of ever making this a truly multicultural, egalitarian culture? I cannot advocate the abandonment of the project; I remain hopeful that eventually we will be able to retain our particular cultural aspects that individualize us while recognizing our commonality.

There have been positive trends in the past few years, even as racism and other forms of intolerance have become more and more acceptable. In the theatre, there has been an increase in the recognition and production of scripts by black playwrights, both male and female. These new plays are not timid, nor do they pretend to be. Suzan-Lori Parks's current popularity has been fueled by two scripts in particular: *Death of the Last Black Man in the Whole Entire World* (1989) and *The America Play* (1993). The plays are not realistic in the strict sense; Parks draws on the historical modes of expression within the African American community in shaping her scripts. Both of these plays have elements of repetition and of a call-and-response form that have descended from West African religious practices through the black church. Parks's *Death of the Last Black Man in the Whole Entire World* uses the "Voice on the TeeVee" to signify the power of the media to influence the actions and beliefs of the other characters, drawing on the complicity of the media in perpetuating racist thought. She includes characters who, while black, have adopted white racist standards. There is Prunes and Prisms, for example, who represents the myth that repeating this particular phrase over and over will reduce large lips. Parks also includes mythological characters like And Bigger and Bigger and Bigger, an obvious reference to the proportions to which Richard Wright's character has grown, and one of the main characters, Black Man with Watermelons, who sits on an electric chair wearing a rope around his neck and holding two watermelons in his hands. He asks repeatedly whether those melons are part of him. Black Woman with Fried Drumstick makes her connections with history through characters like Before Columbus and Queen-Then-Pharaoh-Hatshepsut, and through the historical and repeated deaths of the Black Man, who is killed by lynching and electrocution.

Talvin Wilks's *Tod, the Boy, Tod* (1994) likewise uses traditional African American religious references (the character of Tod's father is a Baptist minister, and Tod is imagined the "savior" of his race) and structure. Wilks's play uses three white businessmen, sitting at a desk above the other characters, to signify the connections between racism and economics. Visually, the three white men in suits sit above and behind the black and Jewish characters, signifying the power structure that attempts to control the actions of the other characters. The primary characters of both plays must face their history before they can move on; Tod comes to understand his blackness through his history.

These plays have in common their dedication to continued struggle against racist oppression. They are only two plays from a larger repertory of contemporary plays by black playwrights, but they both echo the same sentiment. They focus on the cooperation between black men and women, when the recent history is one of infighting between them. Robert Staples said in his study of black women that

> Once Black people are caught up in this intersexual struggle, they will once more become victims of the divide-and-conquer strategy of their real enemy—white racism and its agents. (1973: 5)

Staples dismisses the influence of white feminism as an attempt to divide blacks. Not only do blacks need to overcome the sexism they have learned from white patriarchal culture (particularly that which represents black women as sexually aggressive, or matriarchal, castrating bitches); they must also look to history. History may not be able to shield us from racism, but it can keep us from repeating past mistakes. It may also lead us to adopt solutions that were effective in the past.

For all of these reasons, our history is important. We can see where we might go when we acknowledge where we have been. In looking back specifically at the tradition of black women playwrights, we can see a consistent resistance to the racist icons that were perpetuated by white dominant culture. The persistence and dedication of these women of the past is matched by that of their heirs in the present. One hopes that the publication, production, and classroom study of black women's (and men's) plays and films will continue, so that there will be a better record for those who follow us. In addition, perhaps more black men will join the fight against sexism, which divides the whole black community, and will consciously present images of black women that are not two-dimensional caricatures. The theatre has remained the most promising ground for these types of artistic visions, which unfortunately limits their audience. The expense of producing film has prohibited its recent development (acknowledging that there has always been independent black cinema, it has yet to reach as large an audience as the average Hollywood release). However, it is possible that with the increasing popularity of independent film, more and different black films will be seen by the viewing public. Hand in hand with community efforts, the possibility of real political and social change remains.

Bibliography

Plays

Bonner, Marita. *The Pot Maker*, (1927), in *Wines in the Wilderness: Plays by African American Women from the Harlem Renaissance to the Present*, ed. Elizabeth Brown-Guillory. New York: Greenwood, 1990.

Boucicault, Dion. *The Octoroon, or Life in Louisiana* (1859). Miami: Mnemosyne Publishing Company, 1969.

DeVeaux, Alexis. *The Tapestry* (1976), in *9 Plays by Black Women*, ed. Margaret Wilkerson. New York: New American Library, 1986.

Grimke, Angelina Weld. *Rachel* (1916), in *Black Theatre, U.S.A: Forty-Five Plays by Black Americans, 1847–1974*, ed. James V. Hatch and Ted Shine. New York: Free Press, 1974.

Hammerstein, Oscar II. *Carmen Jones* (1944). New York: Alfred A. Knopf, 1945.

Hansberry, Lorraine. *A Raisin in the Sun* (1959) (30th Anniversary Edition, revised). New York: Samuel French, Inc., 1988.

Hellman, Lillian. *The Little Foxes* (1939). New York: Random House, 1939.

Heyward, Dubose. *Mamba's Daughters* (1929). Garden City, N.J.: Doubleday, Doran, 1929.

———, and Dorothy Heyward. *Porgy* (1924), in *Famous American Plays of the 1920s*, ed. Kenneth Macgowan. New York: Dell, 1959.

Hurston, Zora Neale. *Color Struck* (1925), in *Black Female Playwrights: An Anthology of Plays Before 1950*, ed. Kathy Perkins. Bloomington: Indiana University Press, 1989.

———. *The First One* (1927), in *Black Female Playwrights: An Anthology of Plays Before 1950*, ed. Kathy Perkins. Bloomington: Indiana University Press, 1989.

———, and Dorothy Waring. *Polk County* (1944). Unpublished manuscript, New York Public Library for the Performing Arts, Lincoln Center.

Johnson, Georgia Douglas. *Blue Blood* (1926), in *Black Female Playwrights: An Anthology of Plays Before 1950*, ed. Kathy Perkins. Bloomington: Indiana University Press, 1989.

———. *Blue-Eyed Black Boy* (193?), in *Black Female Playwrights: An Anthology of Plays Before 1950*, ed. Kathy Perkins. Bloomington: Indiana University Press, 1989.

———. *A Sunday Morning in the South* (1926), in *Black Female Playwrights: An Anthology of Plays Before 1950*, ed. Kathy Perkins. Bloomington: Indiana University Press, 1989.

Jones, Lisa. *Combination Skin* (1986), in *Contemporary Plays by Women of Color*, ed. Kathy Perkins and Roberta Uno. New York: Routledge, 1996.

Kennedy, Adrienne. *Funnyhouse of a Negro* (1964) and *The Owl Answers* (1965), in *Adrienne Kennedy In One Act*. Minneapolis: University of Minnesota Press, 1988.

McCullers, Carson. *The Member of the Wedding* (1951). New York: New Directions Publishing Corporation, 1951.

Parks, Suzan-Lori. *The Death of the Last Black Man in the Whole Entire World* (1989), in *The America Play and Other Works*. New York: Theatre Communications Group, 1995.

Rahman, Aisha. *Unfinished Women Cry in No Man's Land While a Bird Dies in a Gilded Cage* (1984), in *Nine Plays by Black Women*, ed. Margaret Wilkerson. New York: New American Library, 1986.

Shange, Ntozake. *for colored girls who have considered suicide/when the rainbow is enuf* (1977). New York: Bantam Books, 1977.

West, Cheryl. *Jar the Floor* (1989), in *Women Playwrights: The Best Plays of 1992*, ed. Robyn Goodman and Marisa Smith. Newbury, Vt.: Smith and Kraus, 1992.

134

Wilks, Talvin. *Tod, the Boy, Tod* (1994). Seattle: Rain City Publications, 1994.

Wolfe, George C. *The Colored Museum* (1986), in *New Plays USA:4*, ed. James Leverett and Gillian Richards. New York: Theatre Communications Group, 1988.

Yordan, Phillip. *Anna Lucasta* (1945). New York: Random House, 1945.

Films

Anna Lucasta, dir. Arnold Lavin. United Artists, 1958.

The Birth of a Nation, dir. D. W. Griffith. 1915.

Carmen Jones, dir. Otto Preminger. 20th Century Fox, 1954.

Corrina, Corrina, dir. Jessie Nelson. New Line Cinema, 1994.

Daughters of the Dust, dir. Julie Dash. Geechee Girls/Kino International, 1991.

Gone With the Wind, dir. Victor Fleming, George Cukor, and Sam Wood. MGM, 1939.

Imitation of Life, dir. John M. Stahl. Universal, 1934.

Imitation of Life, dir. Douglas Sirk. Universal, 1959.

The Making of A Legend: Gone With the Wind, dir. David Hinton. MGM/UA, 1989.

The Member of the Wedding, dir. Fred Zinnemann. Paramount, 1952.

Pinky, dir. Elia Kazan. 20th Century Fox, 1949.

Porgy and Bess, dir. Otto Preminger. Columbia, 1959.

A Raisin in the Sun, dir. Daniel Petrie. Columbia, 1961.

She's Gotta Have It, dir. Spike Lee. Island Pictures, 1986.

Show Boat, dir. James Whale. Universal, 1936.

Books and Journals

Aaron, Daniel. 1983. "The 'Inky Curse': Miscegenation in the White American Literary Imagination," *Social Science Information* 22(2): 169–90.

Alter, Jean. 1990. *A Sociosemiotic Theory of Theatre*. Philadelphia: Pennsylvania University Press.

Anderlini, Serena. 1990. *"colored girls*; A Reaction to Black Machismo, or Hues of Erotic Tension in New Feminist Solidarity?" *Theatre Survey* 2(2): 33–54, Spring.

Anderson, Lisa M. 1996. "From Blackface to Genuine Negroes: Nineteenth Century Minstrelsy and the Icon of the Negro," *Theatre Research International*, 21(1): 17–23, Spring.

Anzaldua, Gloria, ed. 1990. *Making Face, Making Soul/Haciendo Caras: Creative and Critical Perspectives by Feminists of Color*. San Francisco: Aunt Lute Books.

Austin, Gayle. 1990. *Feminist Theories for Dramatic Criticism*. Ann Arbor: Univeristy of Michigan Press.

Barthes, Roland. 1957. *Mythologies*. Paris: Éditions du Seuil.

———. 1977. *Image, Music, Text*, tr. Stephen Heath. New York: Farrar, Straus, and Giroux.

Begley, Sharon. 1995. "Three Is Not Enough," *Newsweek* 125(7): 67–69 February 13.

Bennett, Lerone, Jr. 1988. *Before the Mayflower: A History of Black America*, 6th rev. ed. New York: Penguin Books.

Berzon, Judith. 1978. *Neither White Nor Black: The Mulatto Character in Fiction*. New York: New York University Press.

Betsko, Kathleen, and Rachel Koenig. 1987. *Interviews with Contemporary Women Playwrights*. New York: Beech Tree Books.

Bogle, Donald. 1989. *Toms, Coons, Mulattoes, Mammies, and Bucks: An Interpretive History of Blacks in American Films*. New York: Continuum.

Brassmer, William, ed. 1970. *Black Drama: An Anthology*. Columbus, Ohio: Merrill.

Brown-Guillory, Elizabeth, ed. 1990. *Wines in the Wilderness: Plays by African American Women from the Harlem Renaissance to the Present*. New York: Greenwood Press.

Buckley, Michael. 1994. "The Ladies Who Launch," *Theatre Week* 8(10): 17.

Butler, Judith, and Joan W. Scott, eds. 1990. *Feminists Theorize the Political*. New York: Routledge.

Carby, Hazel. 1987. *Reconstructing Womanhood: The Emergence of the Afro-American Woman Novelist*. New York: Oxford University Press.

Carlson, Marvin. 1990. *Theatre Semiotics: Signs of Life*. Bloomington: Indiana University Press.

Carter, Steven R. 1993. *Hansberry's Drama: Commitment Amid Complexity*. New York: Meridian.

Case, Sue-Ellen. 1988. *Feminism and Theatre*. New York: Methuen.

Cham, Mbyd B., and Claire Andrade-Watkins. 1988. *Blackframes: Critical Perspective on Black Independent Cinema*. Cambridge and London: MIT Press.

Chinoy, Helen Krich, and Linda Walsh Jenkins. 1981. *Women in American Theatre: Careers, Images, Movements*. New York: Crown.

Clarkson, Thomas. 1969. *Slavery and Commerce of the Human Species*. Miami: Mnemosyne.

Collins, Patricia Hill. 1990. *Black Feminist Thought: Knowledge, Consciousness, and the Politics of Empowerment*. New York: Routledge.

Cose, Ellis. 1995. "One Drop of Bloody History," *Newsweek* 125(7): 70–72, February 13.

Cripps, Thomas. 1993a. *Making Movies Black*. New York: Oxford University Press.

———. 1993b. *Slow Fade to Black: The Negro in American Film, 1900–1942*. New York: Oxford University Press.

Dash, Julie. 1992. *Daughters of the Dust: The Making of an African American Woman's Film*. New York: New Press.

Davis, Angela Y. 1983. *Women, Race and Class*. New York: Vintage Books.

———. 1984. *Women, Culture and Politics*. London: Women's Press.

Dent, Gina, ed. 1992. *Black Popular Culture*. Seattle: Bay Press.

Dolan, Jill. 1991. *The Feminist Spectator as Critic*. Ann Arbor: University of Michigan Press.

Donaldson, Laura E. 1992. *Decolonizing Feminisms: Race Gender, and Empire-Building*. Chapel Hill: University of North Carolina Press.

137

Dubey, Madhu. 1994. *Black Women Novelists and the Nationalist Aesthetic.* Bloomington: Indiana University Press.

—. 1929. *The Souls of Black Folk.* Chicago: McClurg.

Du Bois, W. E. B. 1971. *The Seventh Son: The Thought and Writings of W. E. B. Du Bois,* ed. Julius Lester. New York: Random House.

Du Cille, Ann. 1993. "Blue Notes on Black Sexuality," *Journal of the History of Sexuality* 3: 418–44.

Equiano, Olaudah. 1967. *Equiano's Travels: His Autobiography; The Interesting Narrative of the Life of Olaudah Equiano or Gustavus Vassa the African,* ed. Paul Edwards. Portsmouth, N.H.: Heinemann.

Fabre, Genevieve. 1983. *Drumbeats, Masks, and Metaphor,* tr. Melvin Dixon. Cambridge, Mass.: Harvard University Press.

Fanon, Franz. 1967. *Black Skin, White Masks,* tr. Charles Lam Markmann. New York: Grove Press.

—. 1967. *Toward the African Revolution,* tr. Haakon Chevalier. New York: Grove Press.

Flynn, Joyce, and Joyce Occomy Stricklin, eds. 1987. *Frye Street and Environs.* Boston: Beacon Press.

Gates, Henry Louis, ed. 1990. *Reading Black, Reading Feminist.* New York: Penguin Books.

Giddings, Paula. 1984. *When and Where I Enter: The Impact of Black Women on Race and Sex in America.* New York: Morrow.

Gilbert, Douglas. 1943. Untitled interview with Zora Neale Hurston, *World Telegram,* February 1.

Gilman, Sander. 1985a. "Black Bodies, White Bodies: Toward an Iconography of Female Sexuality in Late 19th Century Art, Medicine, and Literature," *Critical Inquiry* 13: 1(204–42).

—. 1985b. *Difference and Pathology: Stereotypes of Sexuality, Race and Madness.* Ithaca: Cornell University Press.

Gilmer, Chris. 1992. "An Interview with Ruby Dee," *Studies in American Drama 1945–Present* 7(2): 241–51.

Goldberg, David Theo. 1993. *Racist Culture: Philosophy and the Politics of Meaning.* London: Basil Blackwell.

138

————, ed. 1990. *Anatomy of Racism*. Minneapolis: University of Minnesota Press.

Gordon, Lewis R. 1995a. *Bad Faith and Antiblack Racism*. Atlantic Highlands, N.J.: The Humanities Press.

————. 1995b. "Critical 'Mixed Race'?" *Social Identities* 1(2): 381–95.

————. 1996a. *Fanon and the Crisis of European Man*. New York: Routledge.

————. 1996b. "Race, Gender, and the Matrices of Desire," in *Sex/Race*, ed. Naomi Zack. New York: Routledge.

Gutman, Herbert. 1976. *The Black Family in Slavery and Freedom*. New York: Vintage.

Haizlip, Shirlee Taylor. 1995. "Passing," *Forbes American Heritage* 46(1): 46–54, March.

Hamalian, Leo, and James V. Hatch, eds. 1991. *The Roots of African American Drama: An Anthology of Early Plays, 1858–1938*. Detroit: Wayne State University Press.

Hart, Lynda, and Peggy Phelan, eds. 1993. *Acting Out: Feminist Performances*. Ann Arbor: University of Michigan Press.

Hatch, James V., and Ted Shine, eds. 1974. *Black Theatre, U.S.A.: Forty-Five Plays by Black Americans, 1847–1974*. New York: Free Press.

Hay, Samuel A. 1994. *African American Theatre: An Historical and Critical Analysis*. Cambridge: Oxford University Press.

Hemenway, Robert E. 1980. *Zora Neale Hurston: A Literary Biography*. Urbana and Chicago: University of Illinois Press.

Hill, Errol, ed. 1987. *The Theatre of Black Americans: A Collection of Critical Essays*. New York: Applause.

hooks, bell. 1992. *Black Looks: Race and Representation*. Boston: South End Press.

————. 1994. *Outlaw Culture: Resisting Representations*. New York: Routledge.

Hughes, Langston, and Milton Meltzer. 1990. *Black Magic: A Pictorial History of the African-American in the Performing Arts*. New York: Da Capo Press.

139

Hull, Gloria T., et al., eds. 1982. *All the Women Are White, All the Blacks Are Men, But Some of Us Are Brave: Black Women's Studies*. Old Westbury, N.Y.: Feminist Press.

———. 1987. *Color, Sex, and Poetry: Three Women Writers of the Harlem Renaissance*. Bloomington: Indiana University Press.

Hurston, Zora Neale. 1942. *Dust Tracks on a Road: An Autobiography*. Philadephia: J. B. Lippincott.

Isaacs, Edith. 1947. *The Negro in the American Theatre*. New York: Theatre Arts.

Israel, Lee. 1994. "A Little Grit: Race and *Show Boat*," *Theater Week* 8(10).

James, Stanlie M., and Abena P. A. Busia. 1993. *Theorizing Black Feminisms: The Visionary Pragmatism of Black Women*. New York: Routledge.

Johnson, Beverly. Unpublished manuscript on Edith Goodall Wilson.

Jones, Jacquie. 1994. "Race and Racism: A Symposium," *Social Text* 42: 12.

Jones, Lisa. 1994. *Bulletproof Diva: Tales of Race, Sex, and Hair*. New York: Doubleday.

Joseph, Gloria I., and Jill Lewis. 1981. *Common Differences: Conflicts in Black and White Feminist Perspectives*. Boston: South End Press.

Kennedy, Adrienne. 1989. *People Who Led To My Plays*. New York: Theatre Communications Group.

Keyssar, Helene. 1981. *The Curtain and the Veil: Strategies in Black Drama*. New York: Burt Franklin.

Kintz, Linda. 1992. "The Sanitized Spectacle," *Theatre Journal* 44(1): 67–86, March.

Klein, Joe. 1995. "The End of Affirmative Action," *Newsweek* 125(7): 36–37, February 13.

Kreuger, Miles. 1977. *Show Boat: The Story of a Classic American Musical*. New York: Oxford University Press.

Lerner, Gerda. 1972. *Black Women in White America: A Documentary History*. New York: Pantheon Books.

140

Lester, Neal A. 1990. "An Interview with Ntozake Shange," *Studies in American Drama 1945–Present* 5: 42–66.

Macgowan, Kenneth, ed. 1959. *Famous American Plays of the 1920s.* New York: Dell.

Mahone, Sydne. 1994. *Moon Marked and Touched by Sun.* New York: Theatre Communications Group.

Mast, Gerald, and Marshall Cohen, eds. 1985. *Film Theory and Criticism: Introductory Readings.* 3rd ed. New York: Oxford University Press.

Morganthau, Tom. 1995. "What Color Is Black?" *Newsweek* 125(7): 63–65, February 13.

Morrison, Toni. 1992. *Playing in the Dark: Whiteness and the Literary Imagination.* Cambridge: Harvard University Press.

NAACP, Washington, D.C. 1916. Program, *Rachel*, courtesy of the Billy Rose Theatre Collection, New York Public Library, Lincoln Center.

Nederveen Pieterse, Jan. 1992. *White on Black: Images of Africa and Blacks in Western Popular Culture.* New Haven: Yale University Press.

Nelson, Cary, and Lawrence Grossberg, eds. 1988. *Marxism and the Interpretation of Culture.* Urbana: University of Illinois Press.

Nemiroff, Robert, ed. 1987. *A Raisin in the Sun (Expanded Twenty-fifth Anniversary Edition) and The Sign in Sidney Brustein's Window.* New York: New American Library.

———. 1970. *To Be Young, Gifted, and Black: Lorraine Hansberry in Her Own Words.* New York: New American Library.

Oshana, Maryann. 1985. *Women of Color: A Filmography of Minority and Third World Women.* New York: Garland.

Patterson, Lindsay, ed. 1967. *Anthology of the American Negro in the Theatre: A Critical Approach.* New York: Publishers.

Perkins, Kathy A., ed. 1989. *Black Female Playwrights: An Anthology of Plays Before 1950.* Bloomington: Indiana University Press.

———, and Roberta Uno, eds. 1996. *Contemporary Plays by Women of Color.* New York: Routledge.

Peterson, Bernard L., Jr., ed. 1990. *Early Black American Playwrights and Dramatic Writers: A Biographical Directory and Catalog of Plays, Films, and Broadcast Scripts*. New York: Greenwood Press.

Rainwater, Lee, and William L. Yancey. 1967. *The Moynihan Report and the Politics of Controversy*. Cambridge: MIT Press.

Reilly, Charlie. 1994. *Conversations with Amiri Baraka*. Jackson: University of Mississippi Press.

Reinelt, Janelle G., and Joseph R. Roach. 1992. *Critical Theory and Performance*. Ann Arbor: University of Michigan Press.

Richardson, Willis, ed. [1930] 1993. *Plays and Pageants from the Life of the Negro*. Reprint Jackson: University Press of Mississippi.

Roach, Joseph R. 1992. "Mardi Gras Indians and Others: Genealogies of American Performance," *Theatre Journal* 44(4): 461–83.

Roberts, Diane. 1994. *The Myth of Aunt Jemima: Representations of Race and Region*. New York: Routledge.

Sharpley-Whiting, T. Denean, and Renée T. White, eds. 1997. *Spoils of War*. Lanham, Md.: Rowman & Littlefield.

Smith, Susan Harris. 1988. "An Interview with Charles Gordone," *Studies in American Drama 1945–Present* 3: 127.

Snead, James. 1994. *White Screens/Black Images: Hollywood from the Dark Side*. New York: Routledge.

Staples, Robert. 1973. *The Black Woman in America: Sex, Marriage, and the Family*. Chicago: Nelson Hall.

Stubbs, Carolyn A. 1978. *Angelina Weld Grimke: Washington Poet and Playwright*. Ph.D. Dissertation, George Washington University.

Takaki, Ronald. 1993. *A Different Mirror: A History of Multicultural America*. Boston: Little, Brown.

Tate, Claudia. 1983. *Black Women Writers At Work*. New York: Continuum.

Thompson, Peter, ed. 1984. *Plays of Dion Boucicault*. Cambridge: Cambridge University Press.

Toll, Robert C. 1974. *Blacking Up: The Minstrel Show in Nineteenth-Century America*. New York: Oxford University Press.

Turner, S. H. Regina. 1982. *Images of Black Women in the Plays of Black*

Female Playwrights, 1950–1975. Ph.D. Dissertation, Bowling Green State University.

Walker, Alice. 1983. *In Search of Our Mothers' Gardens: Womanist Prose*. New York: Harcourt Brace Jovanovich.

———. 1992. *Possessing the Secret of Joy*. New York: Harcourt Brace.

Wall, Cheryl A. 1993. "Zora Neale Hurston: Changing Her Own Words," in *Zora Neale Hurston: Critical Perspectives Past and Present*, ed. Henry Louis Gates and K. A. Appiah. New York: Amistad Press.

Weiss, Andrea. 1993. *Vampires and Violets: Lesbians in Film*. New York: Penguin.

Wilkerson, Margaret, ed. 1986. *9 Plays by Black Women*. New York: New American Library.

Zack, Naomi. 1993. *Race and Mixed Race*. New York: Routledge.

Index

About the Author

Lisa M. Anderson received her B.A. from Mount Holyoke College, her M.A. from Smith College, and her Ph.D. from the University of Washington. She is an assistant professor of African American studies and theatre at Purdue University, where she teaches courses in dramatic literature and theory, African American theatre history, and critical race theory. She has authored several articles on African American theatre and the iconography of blacks in popular culture.